The Great White Tribe in Filipinia

Paul T. Gilbert

The
Great White Tribe
in
Filipinia

Paul T. Gilbert

Preface

The legendary white tribe that is said to wander in the mountains of Mindoro is but distantly related to the Great White Tribe now scattered through the greater part of Filipinia. Extending from the Babuyanes off Luzon, to Tawi-Tawi and Sibutu off the coast of Borneo, the Great White Tribe has made its presence felt throughout the archipelago.

The following pages are the record of my own impressions and experiences in the Philippines. The few historical and geographical allusions made have been selected only as they were significant, explanatory, picturesque. A logical arrangement of the chapters will enable the reader to survey the islands as a great bird hovering above might do—will make the map of Filipinia "look like a postage-stamp."

I promise that the reader shall be introduced to all the most important members of the Great White Tribe, as well as to the representatives of races brown and black. We will peep through the hedge together as the savages and pagans execute their grotesque dances or perform their sacrifices to the god of the volcano. Furthermore, the reader shall attend the Oroquieta Ball with Maraquita and Don Julian, or, if he likes, with "Foxy Grandpa" and "The Arizona Babe."

I ought to dedicate this book to many people,—to that wonderful brown baby Primitivo, who has written that he "loves me the most best of all the world;" to "Fresno Bill," that charter member of the Great White Tribe, with whom I have knocked around from Zamboanga to Vigan; or to that coterie of college men in old Manila who extended me so many courtesies while I was there. I send them all my compliments from the homeland, and ask the reader, if he will, to do likewise.

CINCINNATI, OHIO,

December, 1903.

CONTENTS

Illustrations

In Old Manila (River Opposite Custom-House)

Chapter I.
In Old Manila.

As the big white transport comes to anchor three miles out in the green waters of Manila Bay, a fleet of launches races out to meet the messenger from the Far West. The customs officers in their blue uniforms, the medical inspectors, and the visitors in white duck suits and panama hats, taking their ease upon the launches without the slightest sign of curiosity, give one his first impressions of the Oriental life—the white man's easy-going life in the Far East. But the ideas of the newcomer are to undergo a change after his first few days on shore, when he takes up the grind, and realizes that his face is getting pasty—that the cool veranda and the drive on the Luneta do not constitute the entire program, even in Manila.

Unwieldy lighters and strange-looking *cascos* now surround the transport, and the new arrival sees the Filipino for the first time. Under the woven helmet of the nearest *casco* squats a shriveled woman, one of the witches from Macbeth, stirring a blackened pot of rice. A gamecock struggles at his tether in the stern, while the deck amidships swarms with wiry brown men, with bristling pompadours and feet like rubber, with wide-spreading toes. With unintelligible cries they crowd the gunwale, spurning the iron hull of the transport with long billhooks, as the heavy swell sucks out the water, leaving the streaming sluices and the great red hull exposed, and threatening at the inrush of the sea to bump the *casco* soundly against the solid iron plates of the larger ship. A most disreputable-looking crew it is, the ragged trousers rolled up to the knee, the network shirts, or cotton blouses full of holes drawn down outside. Highly excitable, and yet good-natured as they work, they take possession and disgorge the ship, while Chinamen descend the hatchways after dirty clothes.

Off in the hazy distance lies Cavite, or "the port," with its white mist of war ships lying at anchor where the stout Dutch galleons rode, in 1647, to attack the Spanish caravels, retiring only after the Dutch admiral fell wounded mortally; where later, in the nineteenth century, the Spanish fleet put out to meet the white armada, the grim battleships of Admiral Dewey's line. Where now the lazy sailing vessels and the blackened tramps are anchored, lay, in 1593, the hostile Chinese junks, with the barbaric eye daubed on the bows, the gunwales bristling with iron cannon that had scorned the typhoons of the China Sea and gathered in Manila Bay.

This bay has been the scene of history-making since the sixteenth century. Soon after the flotilla of Legaspi landed the first Spanish settlers on the crescent beach around Manila Bay, the little garrison was put to test by the invasion of the Chinese pirate, Li Ma Hong. The memory of that brave defense in which the Spaniards routed the Mongolian invader, even the disaster of that first of May can never drown. In 1582 the little fleet put out against the Japanese corsair, Taifusa, and returned victorious. In 1610 the fleet of the Dutch pirates was destroyed off Mariveles. Those were stirring days when, but a few years later, the armada of Don Juan de Silva left Manila Bay again to test the mettle of the Dutch. Another naval encounter with the Dutch resulted in a victory for Spanish arms in 1620 in San Bernardino Straits. And off Corregidor, whose blue peak marks the entrance to Manila Bay, the Dutchmen were again defeated by the galleons of Don Geronimo de Silva. Now, near the Cavite shore, is seen the twisted wreck of one of the ill-fated men of war that went down under the intolerable fire from Dewey's broad-sides. And in 1899 the Spanish transports left Manila Bay forever under the command of Don Diego de los Rios, with the remnant of the Spanish troops aboard.

The city of Manila lies in a broad crescent, with its white walls and the domes of churches glowing in the sun. On landing at the Anda monument, you find the gray walls and the moss-grown battlements of the old garrison—a winding driveway leading across the swampy moat and disappearing through the mediæval city gate. This portion of Manila, laid out in the sixteenth century by De Legaspi, occupies the territory on the south side of the Pasig River at the mouth. The frowning walls of the *Cuartel de Santiago* loom above the bustling river opposite the customs-house.

Here, where the young American army officers look out expectantly for the arrival of the transport that is to bring them their promotions, or to take them home, Geronimo de Silva was confined for not pursuing the Dutch vessels after the sea fight off Corregidor. The crumbling walls still whisper of intrigue and secrecy. The fort was built in 1587, and became the base of operations, not only against the pirate fleets of the Chinese, the Moros, and the Dutch, but also in the riots of the Chinese and the Japanese that broke out frequently in the old days. At one time twenty thousand Chinamen were beaten back by an alliance of the Spaniards, Japanese, and natives. On this historic ground the treaty was made in 1570 between the Spaniards and the rajas of Manila, Soliman and Lacandola. The walls survived the fire of 1603. The earthquake causing the evacuation of Manila could not shake them. Another prisoner of state, Corcuera, who had fought the Moros in the Jolo Archipelago, was locked up in the *Cuartel de Santiago* at the instance of his Machiavellian successor. In 1642 the fort was strengthened by additional artillery because of an expected visit from the Dutch. Today a soldier in a khaki uniform mounts guard at the street entrance. The courtyard is adorned by pyramids of cannon-balls and tidy rows of *bonga*-trees. The soldiers' quarters line the avenue on either side, and bugle-calls resound where formerly was heard the call of the night watchman.

A number of elaborate but narrow passages—dim, gloomy archways, where the chain and windlass stand dust-covered from disuse—connect the walled town with the extra-muros sections. The *Puerto del Parian*, on the Ermita side, is one of the most imposing of these gates. Near the botanical gardens on the boulevard, at the small booth where Juliana sells cigars and bottled soda, following the turnpike over the moat, you come to the Parian gate, crowned by the Spanish arms, in crumbling bas-relief. Beyond the drawbridge—lowered never to be raised again—where rumbling pony-carts crowd the pedestrians to the wall, the passage opens into gloomy dungeons, with barred windows looking out upon the stagnant waters of the moat. With an involuntary shudder, you pass on. A native policeman, in an opera-bouffe uniform, stands at the further end in order to dispatch the vehicles that can not pass each other in the narrow gate. Windowless, yellow walls, upon the corners of the streets, make reckless driving very dangerous, and collisions frequently occur. A vacant sentry-box stands just within the city walls, and, turning here into the long street, you immediately find yourself in an old Spanish town.

Here the grand churches and the public buildings are located; the cathedral, after the Romano-Byzantine style of architecture; the *Palacio*, built after Spanish notions of magnificence, around a courtyard shaded by rare trees; and many other edifices, used for official and ecclesiastic purposes. The streets are paved with cobblestone and laid out regularly in squares, in accordance with the plan of De Legaspi, so that one side or the other will be always in the shade. Beautiful plazas, with their palms and statues, frequently relieve the glare of the white walls. The sidewalks are narrow, and are sheltered by projecting balconies.

The heavily-barred windows, ponderous doors, and quaint signboards give the streets an old-world aspect, while *Calle Real* is spanned by an arched gallery, like the Venetian Bridge of Sighs. Tailor-shops, laundries, restaurants, and barber-shops, where swinging punkas waft the odor of bay rum through open doors, suggest a scene from some forgotten story-book or the stage-setting for an Elizabethan play. In the commercial streets the absence of show-windows will be noticed. Bookstores display their wares on stands outside, while of the contents of the other shops, one can obtain no adequate idea until he enters through the open doors. The interesting signboards, whether they can be interpreted or not, tend to excite the curiosity. *"Los Dos Hermanos"* (The Two Brothers) is a tailor-shop, a *Sastreria*; and the shoestore a *Zapateria*. The family grocery-store, *El Globo*, is advertised by a huge globe, battered from long years of service; and *La Lira,* or the music-store, may be known by the sign of the gold lyre.

These streets have been the scene of many a drama in the past. Earthquakes in 1645, in 1863, and 1880, caused great loss of life and property. The plague broke out in 1628, when Spaniards, Filipinos, and Chinese were swept off indiscriminately. Later, epidemics of smallpox and cholera have made a prison and a pesthouse of Manila. Only in 1902 the city suffered from a run of cholera, and the Americans, in spite of all precautions, could not stop the spread of the disease. The streets were flushed at night; districts of native houses were put to the torch, and the detention-camp was full of suffering humanity. The natives, in their ignorance, went through the streets in long processions, carrying the images of saints, chanting, and burning candles, and at night would throw the bodies of the dead into the river or the canal. The ships lay wearily at quarantine out in the bay, and the chorus of bells striking the hour at night was heard over the quiet waters. Officers patrolled the streets, inspected drains and cesspools where the filth of ages had collected, giving the forgotten corners of Manila such a cleaning as they never had received before.

But there were days of triumph and rejoicing—days such as had come to Greece and Rome; days when the level of life was raised to heights of inspiration. Not only have the streets re-echoed to the martial music of the victorious Americans when Governor Taft or the vice-governor were welcomed, but the town had rung with shouts of triumph when provincial troops had come back from the conquest of barbarians, or when the fleets returned from victories over the Dutch and English and the Moro pirates of the southern archipelago. And the streets reverberated to the sound of drum and trumpet when, in 1662, the special companies of guards were organized to put down the rebellion of the Chinese in the suburbs. But in 1762 the town capitulated to the English, and the occupation by Americans more than a century later, was a repetition of the scenes enacted then.

Because of the volcanic condition of the island, the houses can not be built more than two stories high. The ground floor is of stone, and contains, besides the storehouse or a suite of living rooms, the stables, arranged around a tiled courtyard, where the carriages are washed. A broad stairway conducts to the main corridor above. The floor, of polished hardwood, is uncarpeted and scrupulously clean. Each morning the *muchachos* (house-boys) mop the floor with kerosene, skating around the room on rags tied to their feet, or pushing a piece of burlap on all fours across the floor. The walls are frescoed pink and blue; the ceiling is often of painted canvas. The windows, fitted with translucent shell in tiny squares, slide back and forth, so that the balcony can be thrown open to the light. Double walls, making an alcove on one side, keep out the heat of the ascending or descending sun. The balcony at evening is a favorite resort, and visitors are entertained in open air. In the interior arrangement of the houses, little originality is shown, the Spaniards having insisted upon merely formal principles of art. The stiff arrangement of the chairs, facing each other in precise rows, as if a conclave were about to be held, does not invite conviviality. There are few pictures on the walls,—a faded chromo, possibly, in a gilt frame, representing some old-fashioned prospect of Madrid, or the tinted portrait of the royal family.

The Spanish residents and the *mestizos* entertain with great politeness and formality. Five o'clock is the fashionable hour for visiting, as earlier in the afternoon the family is liable to be in *négligée*. The Spanish women, in loose, morning gowns, or blouses, and in flapping slippers, present a rather slovenly appearance during morning hours; also the children, in their "union" suits, split tip the back, impress the stranger as untidy. During the noon *siesta* everybody goes to sleep, to come to life late in the afternoon. At eight o'clock the chandelier is lighted and the evening meal is served. This is a very formal dinner, consisting of innumerable courses of the same thing cooked in different styles. A glass of *tinto* wine, a glass of water, and a toothpick whittled by the loving hands of the *muchacho*, finishes the meal. The kitchen is located in the rear, and generally overlooks the court, and near by are the bathroom and the laundry.

In the walled city small hotels are numerous, their entryways well banked with potted palms. The usual stone courtyard, damp with water, is surrounded by the pony-stalls, where dirty stable-boys go through their work mechanically, smoking cigarettes. The dining-room and office occupy most of the second floor. This is the library, reception-room, and ladies' parlor, all in one; the guest-rooms open into this apartment. These are very small, containing a big Spanish tester-bed, with a cane bottom, and the other necessary furniture. The sliding windows open out into the street or the attractive courtyard, and the room reminds you somewhat of an opera-box. My own room looked out at the hospital of San José, where a big clock, rather weatherbeaten, tolled the hours.

Manila to-day, however, is a contradiction. Striking anachronisms occur from the confusion of Malayan, Asiatic, European, and American traditions. Heavy escort-wagons, drawn by towering army mules, crowd to the wall the fragile *quilez* and the *carromata*(two-wheeled gigs), with their tough native ponies. Tall East Indians, in their red turbans; Armenian merchants, soldiers in khaki uniforms, and Chinese coolies bending under heavy loads, jostle each other under the projecting balconies, while Filipinos shuffle peacefully along the curb.

The new American saloons look rather out of place in such a curious environment, and telegraph wires concentrated at the city wall seem even more incongruous.

Chapter II.
All About the Town.

The wide streets radiating from the Bridge of Spain are lined with lemonade stands, where the cube of ice is sheltered from the sun by striped awnings. Leaving the walled town on the river side—the gate has been destroyed by earthquakes—you can take the ferry over to the Tondo side. The ferryboat is a round-bottomed, wobbly sampan, with a tiny cabin in the stern. You crouch down, waiting for the boat to roll completely over, which at first it seems inclined to do, or try to plan some method of escape in case the pilot gets in front of one of the swift-moving tugs. You have good reason to congratulate yourself on being landed at a stone-quay in a tangle of small launches, ferryboats, and *cascoes*. The Tondo Canal may be crossed on a covered barge, poled by an ancient boatman, who collects the fares—a copper cent of Borneo, Straits Settlements, or Hong Kong coinage—much in the same way as the pilot of the Styx collects the obolus.

Under the long porch of the customs-house, a dummy engine noisily plies up and down among the long-horned carabaos and piles of merchandise. Types of all nations are encountered here. The immigration office swarms with Chinamen herded together, rounded up by some contractor. Every Chinaman must have his photograph, his number, and description in the immigration officer's possession. Indian merchants, agents of the German, Spanish, and English business firms are looking after new invoices. A party of American tourists, just arrived from China, are awaiting the inspection of their baggage.

The Bridge of Spain, that famous artery of commerce, over which a stream of carabao-carts, crowded tram-cars, pleasure vehicles, and army wagons flows continuously, spans the Pasig River at the head of the Escolta in Binondo. Here the bazaars and European business houses are located, while the avenues that branch off lead to other populous and swarming districts. *La Extrameña*, a grocery and wine-store; *La Estrella del Norte*— "The North Star"—diamond and jewelry-store; the *Sombreria*, hatstore, advertised by a huge wooden hat hung out above the street; and a tobacco booth, are situated on the corners where the bridge and the Escolta meet. The Metropolitan policeman—one of the tall *Americanos* uniformed in khaki riding-breeches and stiff leggings—who, in former days, controlled the traffic of the street, is now supplanted by a Filipino comic-opera policeman. Very few of the old "Mets" are left. It was a body of picked men, the finest soldiers in the volunteer troops, and the most efficient police force in the world. This officer on the Escolta used to be a genius in his line. When balky Filipino ponies blocked the traffic in the crowded thoroughfare, it was this officer that straightened out the tangle. If the tram-car happened to run off the track, it was the "Met" who showed the driver how to put it on again.

The river above the bridge is lined with latticed balconies; but from the veranda of the Paris Restaurant, when that establishment was in its glory, one could sit for hours and watch the bustling river life below. The thatched tops of the huddled *cascos* formed a compact roof that extended half across the stream. Upon these nondescript craft hundreds of Filipinos dwelt, doing their washing and their cooking on the decks. The scanty clothes are hanging out to dry on lines, while naked brats are splashing in the dirty water, clinging to the tightened hawser.

All About the Town (The Tops of Cascoes)

9

Launches go scudding under the low bridge, rending the air with vicious toots. Unwieldly *cascos* are poled down the river, laden heavily with cocoanuts and hemp. Small floating islands whirl along in the swift current, and are carried out to sea. At the *Muelle del Rey*—the "King's Dock"—lie the inter-island steamers, and the gangs of laborers are busy loading and unloading them. Carabao drays are hauling fragrant cargoes of tobacco and Manila hemp, while over the gangplank runs a chain of men, gutting the warehouse of its merchandise. The captain of the *Romulus* stands on the bridge, daintily smoking a cigarette, and supervising the disposal of the demijohns of *tinto* wine. The derrick keeps up an incessant racket as the hold is gradually filled. Although the *Romulus* is advertised to sail to-day at noon, she is as liable to sail at ten o'clock, or possibly to-morrow afternoon; and although bound for Iloilo or Cebu, you can not be at all sure what her destination really is. She may return after a month from a long rambling cruise among the southern isles. The Spanish mariners, in rakish Tam o'Shanter caps, lounge at the entrance to the warehouse, or the office of the *Compania Maritima*, dreamily smoking cigarettes, sometimes imperiously ordering the laborers to *"sigue, hombre!"* (get along!) a warning that the Filipino has grown too familiar with to heed.

Armenian and Indian bazaars, where ivory and the rich fabrics of the Orient are sold; cafés and drugstores, harness-shops, tobacco-shops, and drygoods-stores, emporiums of every kind,—are found on the Escolta, where the prices would astonish any one not yet accustomed to the manners of the Far East. During the morning hours the *quilez* and the *carromata* rattle along the bumpy cobblestones, the native driver, or *cochero*, in a white shirt, smoking a cigarette, and resting his bare feet upon the dashboard. Behind the curtain of a passing *quilez* you can catch a glimpse of brown eyes, raven hair, and olive-tinted cheeks, displayed with all the coquetry of a Manila belle. A Filipino family in a rickety cart, tilted at an impossible angle, are drawn by a moth-eaten pony, mostly bones. Public conveyances—if these are not indeed a myth—are most exasperating. You can never find one when you want it, even at the "Public Carriage Station." If by chance you come across one in the street, the driver will ignore your signal and drive on. Evidently he selects this walk in life merely to discharge the obligations of his conscience, for he never seems to want a passenger, nor will he take one till he finds his vehicle possessed by strategy. The gamins of the corner offer eagerly to find a *carromata* for you, but they frequently forget the object of their mission in their search. Sometimes, when you have ceased to think about a *carromata*, one of these small ragamuffins will pursue you, with a sheepish-looking coachman and disreputable vehicle in tow. Then twenty boys crowd round and claim rewards for having found a rig for you; as they all look alike, you toss a ten-cent piece among the crowd and let them fight it out among themselves.

The driver will begin by making some objection. He will ask to be discharged at noon, or he will make you promise not to turn him over to another *Americano*. When the preliminary arrangements are completed, lighting his cigarette, he cramps himself up in the box, and, maintaining a continual clucking, larrups his skinny pony as the crazy gig goes rocking down the street. The driver never seems to know the town; even the post-office and the Bridge of Spain are *terra incognita* to him. And so you guide him, saying "*silla*," left, or "*mano*," right, "*direcho*," straight ahead, and "'*spera*," stop. You must be careful when you stop, however, as while you are busy with your purchases, your man is liable to run away. While, as a general rule, he shakes his head at the repeated inquires of "*ocupato?*" (taken?) even though the carriage may not be engaged, if some one more unscrupulous or desperate should step in, you would find yourself without a rig. And the result would be the same if dinner-time came round, and he had not had "*sow sow*." Even the fact that he had not collected any fare would not deter him from his resolution.

Is it any wonder, then, that, after all these difficulties, no complaint is made against the rickety, slat-seated carts, with wheels that seem to bar the entrance of the passenger; against the sorry-looking *quilez*,— that attenuated two-wheeled 'bus, where the four passengers must sit with interwoven legs, getting the more implicated as the cart goes bounding on? No; the Americans are glad enough to ride in almost any kind of vehicle. But you must be good-natured, even though the cab is tilted at an angle of some thirty-odd degrees, and even though, in getting out, which is accomplished from the *quilez* in the rear, you lift the tiny pony off his feet. It is enough to take the breath away to ride in one of these conveyances through the congested portions of

Manila. Not only does the turning to the left seem strange, but taking the sharp corners—an accomplishment for which the two-wheeled gig is well adapted—frequently comes near precipitating a collision; and, in order to avoid this, the driver pulls the pony to his haunches. When the coast is clear, you will go rattling merrily away, the *quilez* door, unfastened, swinging back and forth abandonedly, regardless of appearances. It is impossible to satisfy the driver on discharging him, unless by paying him three times the fee. The stranger in Manila, counting out the unfamiliar *media pesos* and *pesetas*, never knows when he has paid enough. Whether to pay his fifteen cents, American or Mexican, for the first hour, and ten cents, or *centavos*, for the hour succeeding, and how many *media pesetas* make a quarter of a dollar in our currency,—these are the questions that annoy and puzzle the newcomer, till he learns to disregard expense, and order his livery from the hotels or private stables.

At noon the corrugated iron blinds of the shops are pulled down; all the carriages have disappeared; the only sign of life in the Escolta is the comical little tram-car, loaded down with little brown men dressed in white, the driver tooting a toy horn, and all the passengers dismounting to assist the car uphill.

The banking center of Manila, built around a dusty plaza in the Tondo district, and consisting of low buildings occupied by offices of shipping and commercial companies, suggests a scene from "The Merchant of Venice" or "Othello." English firms—such as Warner, Barnes & Co.; Smith, Bell & Co.; the Hong Kong-Shanghai Banking Corporation, where the silver *pesos* jingle as the deft clerks stack them up or handle them with their small spades—are situated hereabouts.

Near by, and on an emerald plaza, stand the buildings of the Insular Tobacco Company and of the Oriente Hotel. These buildings are the finest modern structures in Manila. Carriages are waiting in the street in front of the hotel, and at the entrance may be seen a group of army officers in khaki uniform, in white and gold, or—very much more modern—olive drab. The dining-room is entered through the rustling bead-work curtain. Here the Chinese waiters, in long gowns glide noiselessly around.

But the Rosario, where opium-saturated Chinamen sit tailor-fashion at the entrance to their little stalls—where narrow galleries and alleys swarm with Chinese life—is one of the most interesting and complex: of all Manila's thoroughfares. On one side of the street the drygoods-shops are shaded from the sun by curtains in broad stripes of blue and white. The dreamy merchant sits barelegged on the doorsill, and is not to be disturbed by the mere entrance of a purchaser. The opposite side is lined with *Chino* hardware stores, and in each one of them the stock is just the same. These shops supply the stock of merchandise to the provincial agents; for an intricate feudal system is maintained among the Chinese of the archipelago. The rich Manila merchants who have seen their fellow-countrymen safe through from China, and have furnished goods on credit, reap the profits like so many Oriental Shylocks.

At four o'clock the shopping begins again in the Escolta. Apparently the whole town has turned out for a ride. Since the Americans have come, odd sights have been seen in Manila,—cavalry horses harnessed to pony vehicles, phaetons drawn by Filipino ponies, and victorias, intended for a pair of native horses, hastily converted into surreys. Not only do the Spanish women come out in their black *mantillas*, but the Filipino belles and the *mestiza*, girls, in their stiff dresses of *josé* and *piña* cloth. A carriage-load of painted cheeks and burnished pompadours of Japanese frail sisterhood drives by upon its way to the Luneta. Army officers in white dress uniform, the wives and daughters of the officers, bareheaded and in dainty gowns, stop off at Clark's for lemonade, ice-cream, and candy. Soldiers and sailors strolling along the street, or driving rickety native carts, enjoy themselves after the manner of their kind. A brace of well-kept ponies, tugging like game fish, trot briskly away with jingling harness, with the coachman and the footman dressed in white, a foreign consul lounging in the cushions of the neat victoria. A private *carruaje*, drawn by a sleek pony, hastens along, the tiny footman clinging on for dear life to the extension seat behind.

After the whirl on the Luneta, where the military band plays as the oddly-assorted carriages go circling round like fixtures on a steam carousal, the pleasure-seekers leave the driveway on the sea deserted; soldiers and citizens vacate the green benches, and adjourn for dinner. The Spanish life is best seen at the Metropole, where *señors, señoritas,* and *señoras,* exquisitely gowned, sip cognac and coffee at the little tables, carrying on an animated conversation, with expressive flashes of bright eyes or gestures with elaborately-jeweled hands.

Below, in the Luzon café, the Rizal orchestra is playing the impassioned Spanish waltzes, *"Sobre las Olas," "La Paloma,"* to the click of billiard balls and the guffaws of soldiers. When the evening program ends with *"Dixie,"* every soldier in a khaki uniform—bronzed, grizzled fellows, many of them back from some campaign out in the provinces—will rise immediately to his feet, respectfully remove his hat, and as the music that reminds him of the home-land swells and gathers volume, fill the corridors with cheer upon cheer as the lights are put out; then the sleeping coachman rouses himself, and starts the reluctant pony on the journey home.

Chapter III.
The White Man's Life.

It happened that my first home in Manila was a temporary one, shared with a hundred others, at the *nipa* barracks at the Exposition grounds. Who of all those that were similarly situated will forget the long row of mimosa-trees that made a leafy archway over the cool street; or the fruit merchants squatting beside the bunches of bananas and the tiny oranges spread out upon the ground? There was the pink pavilion where that enterprising Chinaman, Ah Gong, conducted his indifferent restaurant. After these many days I can still hear the clatter of the plates, the jingle of the knives and forks, placed on the tables by the Chinese waiters. There was the crowd on the veranda waiting for the second table, opening their correspondence as they waited. And what an indescribable sensation was imparted on receiving the first letter in a foreign land!

The long, cool barrack-rooms were swept by the fresh breezes. Here, in the bungalow, the army cots had been arranged in rows and covered by mosquito-bars suspended from the wires stretched overhead. When tucked inside of the mosquito-bar, one felt as though he were a part of a menagerie. "*Muchacho*" was the first new word you learned. It was advisable to call for a *muchacho* often, even though you did not need his services, in order to exploit your own experience and your superiority. And here you were first cheated by the wily Chinese peddlers—although you had cut them down to half their price—when they unrolled their packs of crêpe pajamas, network underwear, and other merchandise.

And all one Sunday afternoon you listened to a lecture from the President of the Manila Board of Health, who told of the diseases that the flesh was heir to in the Philippines, and cheerfully assured you that within a month or two your weight would be reduced to the extent of twenty-five or fifty pounds. And after dinner—where you learned that *chiquos* though they looked a good deal like potatoes, were a kind of fruit—while you were strolling down the avenue beyond the markethouse, you got a ducking from a sudden shower that ceased quite as unceremoniously as it had begun. There was excitement in the bungalow that night because of its invasion by a hostile monkey. An impromptu vigilance committee finally succeeded in ejecting the unwelcome visitor, persuading him of the superior advantages of "Barracks B."

Together with a few dissenters, I moved out next morning, finding better quarters in the first floor of a Spanish house in Magallanes. We made the best of an old ruin opposite, which we considered picturesque, and which was occupied by Filipino squatters, who conducted a hand laundry there. Our first *muchacho*, Valentine, surprised us by existing on the ten-cent dinners of the Chinese chophouse on the corner. But he assured us that it was a good place; that the greasy Chinaman, who fried the sausages and boiled the rice back in the tiny den, was a great favorite. At our own restaurant, two Negro women made the best corn-fritters we had ever tasted; a green parrot and a monkey squawked and chattered on the balustrade; a Filipino boy played marches on a cracked piano-forte.

And so we lived behind the heavily-barred windows, watching the shifting throng—the staggering coolies, girls with trays of oranges upon their heads, and men in curiously fashioned hats—driving around the city in the afternoon (for Valentine was at his best in getting *carromatas* under false pretenses) till the little family broke up. The first to go returned after a day or two, almost in tears with the alarming information that the mayor of the town that he had been assigned to was a naked savage; that what he supposed was pepper on the fried eggs he had had for breakfast, had turned out to be black ants—and wouldn't we please pay his *carromata* fare, because he was completely out of funds?

The carabao carts gradually removed our baggage. Valentine was faithful to the last. Most of us met each other later, and exchanged notes. One had escaped the target practice of ladrones; one had been lost among the mountains of Benguet; another had been carried to Manila on a coasting steamer, reaching the Civil hospital in time to fight against the fevers that had wasted him; and poor Fitz died of cholera in one of the most lonely villages among the Negros hills.

"Won't those infernal bells stop ringing for a while and let a fellow go to sleep?" said Howard as he got out of bed. "Look at those creatures, will you?" pointing to the fat mosquitoes at the top of the mosquito-bar. "The vampires! How do you suppose they got in, anyway?"

"It beats me," said the Duke. "It isn't the mosquitoes or the bells: that ball of fire that's shining through the window makes a perfect oven of the room."

The merciless sun had risen over the low roofs of the walled city, and the heat was radiating from the white walls and the scorching streets. The Duke was sitting on the edge of the low army cot in his pajamas and his bedroom slippers, smoking a native cigarette.

"It must be about ten o'clock," said Howard. "I wonder if the Chinaman left any breakfast for us."

"Probably. A couple of cold fried eggs, or a clammy dish of oatmeal and condensed milk. Shall we get up and go somewhere?"

"I can't find any clothes," said Howard; "this place is turning into a regular chaos, anyway." It was indeed a chaos,—lines of clothes where the mosquitoes swarmed, papers and books scattered about the floor, pajamas, duck suits, towels on every chair, and muddy white shoes strewn around. "Doesn't the *muchacho* ever clean things up?"

"That's nothing," said the Duke; "wait till the Chinaman runs off with all your washing. I can lend you a white suit; and, say,—tell the *muchacho* to come in and *blanco* a few shoes."

As there are no apartment-houses in Manila, the young clerk on small salary will usually live in a furnished room in the walled city. For the first few months it is a rather dreary life. The cool veranda and the steamer chair, after the day's work, is a luxury denied the young Americans within the city walls. The list of amusements that Manila offers is an unattractive one. There is a baseball game between two companies of soldiers, or between the Government employees representing different departments. There is the cock-fight out at Santa Ana, Sunday mornings and *fiesta* days; but this is mostly patronized by natives, and is not especially agreeable to Americans. The Country club—reached after a long drive out Malate way, past the Malate fort that bears the marks of Dewey's shells, past the old church once occupied by soldiers, through the rice-pads where the American troops first met the Insurrecto firing line—is little more than a mere gambling-house. It is now visited by those whose former resorts in the walled city have been broken up by the constabulary.

The races of the Santa Mesa Jockey dub are held on Sunday afternoons. It is a rather dusty drive out to the track. A number of noisy "road-houses" along the way, where drinking is going on; the Paco cemetery, where the bleached bones have been piled around the cross,—these are the sole diversions that the road affords. The races are interesting only in the opportunity they offer to observe the native types. Here you will find the Filipino dandy in his polished boots, his low-crowned derby hat, and baggy trousers. He makes the boast that he has not walked fifty meters on Manila's streets in the past year. This dainty little fellow always travels in a carriage. He flicks the ashes off his cigarette with his long finger-nail as he stands by while the gay-colored jockeys are being weighed in. Up in the grandstand, in a private box, a party of *mestiza* girls, elaborately gowned, are sipping lemonade, or eating sherbet and vanilla cakes, while one of the jockeys leans admiringly upon the rail. The silver *pesos* stacked up on the table in the center of the box are given to a man in waiting to be wagered on the various events. The finishes are seldom very close, the Filipino ponies scampering around the turf like rats. A native band, however, adds to the excitement which the clamor at the booking office and the animated chatter of *dueñas*, *caballeros*, jockeys, and *señoritas* in the galleries intensifies.

Manila, the City of churches, celebrates its Sabbath in its own peculiar way. The Protestant churches suffer in comparison with the grand church of San Sebastian—set up from the iron plates made in Belgium—and the churches of the various religious orders. Magnificence and show appeal most strongly to the Filipino. He is taught to look down on the Protestant religion as plebeian; the priests regard the Protestant with condescending superciliousness. Until the transportation facilities can be extended there will be no general coming together of Americans even on Sunday morning, as the colony from the United States is scattered far and wide throughout the city.

As his salary increases, the young Government employee looks around for better quarters. These he secures by organizing a small club and renting the upper floor of one of the large Spanish houses. As the young men in Manila are especially congenial, there is little difficulty in conducting such an enterprise. The members of a lodging club thus formed will generally reserve a table for their use at one of the adjacent boarding-houses or hotels.

The fashionable world—the heads of departments, general army officers, and wealthy merchants—occupy grand residences in Ermita or in San Miguel. These houses, set back in extensive gardens, are approached by driveways banked luxuriously with palms. A massive iron fence, mounted on stone posts, gives to the residence a certain tone of dignity as well as a suggestion of exclusiveness. Those situated in *Calle Real* (Ermita) have verandas, balconies, and summer-houses looking out upon the sea.

The prosperous bachelor has his stable, stable-boys, and Chinese cook. At eight o'clock A. M. the China ponies will be harnessed ready to drive him to the office, and at four o'clock the carriage calls for him to take him home. Most of the Americans thus situated seldom leave their homes. There is, of course, the Army and Navy club in the walled city, and the University club in Ermita; but aside from an occasional visit to these organizations, he is satisfied with a short turn on the Luneta and the privacy of his own house.

The afternoon teas at the University club, where you can see the sunset lighting up Corregidor and glorifying the white battleships, the monthly entertainments at the Oriente, and the governor's reception, are the social features of Manila life. The ladies do considerable entertaining, wearing themselves out in the performance of their social duties. As a relaxation, an informal picnic party will sometimes charter a small launch, and spend the day along the picturesque banks of the Pasig. The customs of Manila make an obligation of a frequent visit to the Civil hospital, if it so happen that a friend is sick there. It is a long ride along *Calle Iris*, with its rows of bamboo-trees, past the merry-go-round, Bilibid prison, and the railway station; but the patients at the hospital appreciate these visits quite sufficiently to compensate for any inconveniences that may have been caused.

During the holiday season, certain attractions are offered at the theaters. While these are mostly given by cheap vaudeville companies that have drifted over from Australia or the China coast, when any deserving entertainment is announced the "upper ten" turn out *en masse*. During the memorable engagement of the Twenty-fourth Infantry minstrels, the boxes at the Zorilla theater were filled by all the pride and beauty of Manila. Captains and lieutenants from Fort Santiago and Camp Wallace, naval officers from the Cavite colony, matrons and maidens from the civil and the military "sets," made a vivacious audience, while the Filipinos packed in the surrounding galleries, applauded with enthusiasm as the cake-walk and the Negro melody were introduced into the Orient.

Where money circulates so freely and is spent so recklessly as in Manila, where the "East of Suez" moral standard is established, the young fellows who have come out to the Far East, inspired by Kipling's poems and the spirit of the Orient, are tempted constantly to live beyond their means. It is a country "where there ain't no Ten Commandments, and a man can raise a thirst." Then the Sampoluc and Quiapo districts, where the carriage-lamps are weaving back and forth among pavilions softly lighted, where the tinkle of the *samosen* is heard, and where O Taki San, immodest but bewitching, stands behind the beadwork curtain, her kimono parted at the knee,—this is the world of the Far East, the cup of Circe.

There was the pathetic case of the young man who "went to pieces" in Manila recently. He was a Harvard athlete, but was physically unsound. As a result of an unfortunate blow received upon the head a short time after his arrival in Manila, he became despondent and morose. After undue excitement he would fall into a dreamy trance. At such times he would fancy that his mother had died, and he would be convulsed with sorrow, breaking unexpectedly into a rousing college song. He meditated suicide, and was prevented several times from taking his own life. On coming to Manila from the provinces, he stoutly refused to be sent home, but lived at his friends' expense, trying to borrow money from everybody that he met. Other young fellows overwhelmed by debts have tried to break loose from the Islands, but have been brought back from Japanese ports to be placed in Bilibid. That is the saddest life of all—in Bilibid. Many a convict in that prison, far away, has been a gentleman, and there are mothers in America who wonder why their boys do not come home.

Somebody once said that Manila life was a perpetual farewell. The days of the arrival and departure of the transports are the days that vary the monotony. As the procession of big mail-wagons rumbles down the Escolta to the post-office, as the letters from America are opened, as the last month's newspapers and magazines appear in the shop-windows, comes a moment of regret and lonesomeness. But as the transport, with its tawny load of soldiers and of joyful officers, pulls out, the dweller in Manila, long ago resigned to fate, takes up the grind again.

Sometimes, on Sunday morning, he will take the customs-house launch out to one of the Manila-Hong Kong boats, to see a friend off for the homeland and "God's country." Leaning over the taffrail, while the crowd below is celebrating the departure by the opening of bottles, he will fancy that he, too, is going—till the warning whistle sounds, and it is time to go ashore. The best view of Manila, it is said, is that obtained from the stern deck of an outgoing steamer, as the red lighthouse and the pier fade gradually away. But even after he has reached the "white man's country" some time he may "hear the East a-calling," and come back again.

Chapter IV.
Around the Provinces.

A half century before the founding of Manila, Magellan had set up the cross upon a small hill on the site of Butuan, on the north coast of Mindanao, celebrating the first mass in the new land, and taking possession of the island in the name of Spain. Three centuries have passed since then, and there are still tribes on that island who have never yielded to the influence of Christianity nor recognized the authority of Spain or the United States. Magellan's flotilla sailing north touched at Cebu, where the explorers made a treaty with King Hamabar. The king invited them to attend a banquet, where, on seeing that his visitors were off their guard, he slew a number of them mercilessly, while the rest escaped. On the same spot three hundred and fifty-odd years later, three American schoolteachers were as treacherously slain by the descendants of this Malay king.

Not till the expedition of Legaspi and the Augustine monks visited the shores of the Visayan islands were the natives subjugated, and the finding of the *Santo Niño* (Holy Child) brought this about. Since then the monks and friars, playing on the superstition of the islanders, have managed to control them and to mold them to their purposes. In 1568 a permanent establishment was made at Cebu by the bestowal of munitions, troops, and arms, brought by the galleons of Don Juan de Salcedo. The conquest of the northern provinces began soon after the flotilla of Legaspi came to anchor in Manila Bay.

The idea that Manila or the island of Luzon comprises most of our possessions in the East is one that I have found quite prevalent throughout America. The broken blue line of the coast of Luzon reaches away in a dim contour to the northward for two hundred miles, until the chain of the Zambales Mountains breaks into the flying, wave-lashed islands standing out against the trackless sea. Southern Luzon, the country of Batangas, and the Camarines, extends a hundred miles south of Manila Bay.

In the far north are the rich provinces of Cagayan, Ilocos Norte and Ilocos Sur, Abra, Benguet, and Nueva Viscaya. The land at the sea level produces hemp, tobacco, rice, and cocoanuts; the heavily-timbered mountain slopes contain rich woods, cedar, mahogany, molave, ebony, and ipil. A wonderful river rushes through the mountain cañons, and the famous valley of the Cagayan is formed — the garden of Eden of the Philippines. The peaks of the Zambales are so high that frost will sometimes gather at the tops, while in the upper forests even the flora of the temperate zone is reproduced. Negritos, the primeval savages, run wild in the great wilderness, while cannibals, head-hunters, and other barbaric peoples live but a short distance from the shore.

The islands to the south of Luzon reach in a long chain toward Borneo, a distance of six hundred miles. During a journey to the southern islands a continuous procession of majestic mountains moves by like a panorama—first the misty peaks of the Mindoro coast; and then the wooded group of islands in the Romblon Archipelago, that rises abruptly out of the blue sea. Hundreds of smaller islands, like bouquets, dot the waters off Panay, while the bare ridges of Cebu of the Plutonic peaks of Negros loom up far beyond. Passing the triple range of Mindanao, the scattered islands of the Jolo Archipelago, the Tapul and the Tawi-Tawi groups mark the extreme southern limits of the Philippines.

In nearly all these islands the interior is taken up by various tribes of savages, sixty or seventy different tribes in all, speaking as many different dialects. There are the Igorrotes of the north, who make it their religion, when the fire-tree blooms, to go out on a still hunt after human heads. When one of their tribe dies, the number of fingers that he holds up as he breathes his last expresses the number of heads which his survivors must secure. An Igorrote suitor, too, must pay the price, if he would have his bride, in human heads. The head of his best friend or of his deadliest enemy is equally acceptable; and if his own pate fall in the attempt, he would not be alone among those who have "lost their heads" because of a fair woman.

Although the island of Luzon was settled later than the southern islands, civilization has been more widely disseminated in the north. A railway line connects Manila with Dagupan and the other cities of the distant provinces. Aparri, on the Rio Grande, near its mouth, is the commercial port of Cagayan. The country around is rich in live stock, and is partly under cultivation. During the rainy season, however, the pontoon bridges over the Rio Grande are swept away; the roads become impassable. The raging torrent of the river threatens the inland navigation, while the monsoons on the China Sea make transportation very difficult.

The provinces of North and South Ilocos bristle with dense forests, where not only savages, but deer, wild hogs, and jungle-fowl abound, and where the white man's foot has never been. The natives bring the forest products, pitch, rattan, and the wild honey, to the coast towns, where they can exchange their goods for rice. While in the mountainous regions of the northern part, barbarians too timid to approach the coast are found, most of the pagan natives are of a mixed type. The primitive Negritos, living in these parts, as those also living on the island of Negros and in Mindanao, are of unknown origin—unless they are allied with similar types of pigmies, such as the Sakais of the Malay Peninsula, or the Mincopies of the Andaman Islands in the Indian Ocean. Some anthropologists would even associate them with the black dwarfs in the interior of Africa. These savages live a nomadic life, and seldom come down near the villages. But the mixed tribes, the Negrito-Malay, or the Malay-Japanese, are bolder and more enterprising. The presence of the Japanese and Chinese pirates in this country in the early days has been the cause of many of the eccentric types whose origin, entirely independent from the origin of the Negritos, was Malayan. Here the Ilocanes, or the natives of the better class, the Christians of these provinces, although of Malay origin, belong to a more cultured class of Malay ancestry. They are amenable to Christian influences, and their manners are agreeable and pleasing. They cultivate abundant quantities of sugar, cotton, indigo, rice, and tobacco, and the women weave the famous *Ilocan* blankets that are sold at such a premium in Manila. Vigan, the capital of South Ilocos, has the finest public buildings and the best-kept streets of any of the provincial cities.

Another tribe of people, the Zambales, are to be found toward the center of Luzon. Few Igorrotes, Ilocanes, and Negritos live in the province of Zambales or Pangasinan. Pampanga Province also has its own tribe and a different dialect. Tagalog is spoken around Manila, in Laguna Province, in Batangas, and the Camarines; Visayan is the language of the southern islands.

A monotonous sameness is the characteristic of most of the small Filipino towns. In seeing one you have seen all; you wonder what good can come out of such a Nazareth, and there are very few of the provincial capitals, indeed, that merit a description. Rambling official buildings, made of white concrete and roofed with *nipa* or with corrugated iron; a ragged plaza, with the church and convent, and the long streets lined with native houses; pigs with heads like coal-scuttles; chickens and yellow dogs and naked brats, scabby and peanut-shaped,—such are the first and last impressions of the Filipino town.

We reached Cebu during the rainy season, and it was a little city of muddy streets and tiled roofs. As the transport came to anchor in the harbor, Filipino boys came out in long canoes, and dived for pennies till the last you saw of them was the white soles of their bare feet. And in another boat two little girls were dancing, while the boys went through the manual of arms. A number of tramp steamers, barkentines, and the big Hong Kong boat were lying in the harbor, while the coasting steamers of the Chinese merchants and the smaller hemp-boats lined the docks. As this was our first port in the Visayan group, the difference between the natives here and those of the Far North was very noticeable. There, the volcanic, wiry Tagalog, or the athletic Igorrote savage; here, the easy-going, happy Visayan, carabao-like in his movements, with a large head, enormous mouth and feet.

Along the water front a line of low white buildings ran,—the wholesale houses of the English, Chinese, Spanish, and American commercial firms. The street was full of carabao carts, yoked to their uncomfortable cattle. Agents and merchants, dressed in white, were hurrying to and fro with manifests. Around the corner was a long street blocked with merchandise, and shaded with the awnings of the Chinese stores. There was a little barber-shop in a *kiosko,* where an idle native, crossing his legs and tilting back his chair, abandoned himself to the spirit of a big guitar. The avenue that branched off here would be thronged with shoppers during the busy hours. Here were the retail stores of every description—"The Nineteenth-century Bazaar," the stock of which was every bit as modern as its name— clothing-stores, tailor-shops, restaurants, jewelry-stores, and curio bazaars.

Numerous plazas were surrounded by old Spanish buildings and hotels. The public gardens—if the acre of dried palms and withered grass may so be called—were situated near the water front, and had a band stand for the use of the musicians on *fiesta* days. The racetrack was adjacent to the gardens, and the public buildings faced these reservations. The magnificent old churches, with their picturesque bell towers; the white convent walls, with niches for the statuettes of saints; the colleges and convents,—give to the provincial capital an air of dignity.

The boarding-house, kept by a crusty but good-hearted Englishman, stood opposite the row of porches roofed with heavy tiles, that made *Calle Colon* a colonnade. Across the street was a window in the wall, where the brown-eyed Lucretia used to sell ginger-ale and sarsaparilla to the soldiers. With her waving pompadour, her olive cheeks, and sultry eyes, Lucretia was the belle of all the town. There wasn't a soldier in the whole command who wouldn't have laid down his life for her. And in this land where nothing seemed to be worth while, Lucretia, with her pretty manners and her gentle ways, had a good influence upon the tawny musketeers who dropped in to play a game of dominos or drink a glass of soda with her; and she treated all of them alike.

A monkey chattered on the balcony, sliding up and down the bamboo-pole, or reaching for pieces of bananas which the boarders passed him from the dinner-table. "Have you chowed yet?" asked a grating voice, which, on a negative reply, ordered a place to be made ready for me at the table. Barefooted *muchachos* placed the thumb-marked dishes on the dirty table-cloth. I might add that a napkin had been spread to cover the spot where the tomato catsup had been spilled, and that the chicken-soup, in which a slice of bread was soaked, slopped over the untidy thumb that carried it. But I omitted this course, as the red ants floating on the surface of the broth rendered the dish a questionable delicacy. The boarders had adjourned to the parlor, and were busy reading "Diamond Dick," "Nick Carter," and the other five and ten cent favorites. A heavy rain had set in, as I drew my chair up to the light and tried to lose myself in the adventures of the boy detective.

But the mosquitoes of Cebu! The rainy season had produced them by the wholesale, and full-blooded ones at that. These were the strange bed-fellows that made misery that night, as they discovered openings in the mosquito-bar that, I believe, they actually made themselves! The parlor (where the bed was situated) was a very interesting room. There was a rickety walnut cabinet containing an assortment of cobwebby Venus's fingers, which remind you of the mantel that you fit over the gas jet; seashells that had been washed up, appropriately branded "Souvenir of Cebu;" tortoise-shell curios from Nagasaki, and an album of pictures from Japan. The floor was polished every morning by the house-boys, and the furniture arranged in the most formal manner, *vis-á-vis*.

The *señorita* Rosario, the sister-in-law of the proprietor, came in to entertain me presently, dressed in a bodice of blue *piña*, with the wide sleeves newly starched and ironed, and with her hair unbound. She sat down opposite me in a rocking-chair, shook off her slippers on the floor, and curling her toes around the rung, rocked violently back and forth. She punctuated her remarks by frequent clucks, which, I suppose, were meant to be coquettish. Her music-teacher was expected presently; so while I wrote a letter on her *escritorio*, the *señorita* smoked a cigarette upon the balcony. The *maestro* came at last; a little, pock-marked fellow, dapper, and neatly dressed, his fingers stained with nicotine from cigarettes. Together they took places at the small piano, and I could see by their exchange of glances that the music-lesson was an incidental feature of the game. They sang together from a Spanish opera the song of Pepin, the great braggadocio, of whom 't is said, when he goes walking in the streets, "the girls assemble just to see him pass."

> "Cuando me lanzo a calle
> Con el futsaque y el cla,
> Todas las niñas se asoman

Solo por ver me pasar:
Unas a otras se dicen
Que chico mas resa lao!
De la sal que va tirando
Voy a coher un punao."

When the music-teacher had departed, the *señorita* leaned out of the balcony, watching the crowd of beggars in the street below. Of all the beggars of the Orient, those of Cebu are the most clinging and persistent and repulsive. Covered with filthy rags and scabs, with emaciated bodies and pinched faces, they are allowed to come into the city every week and beg for alms. Their whining, "*Da mi dinero, señor, mucho pobre me*" ("Give me some money, sir, for I am very poor"), sounds like a last wail from the lower world.

It was at Iloilo that we took a local excursion steamer across to the *pueblo* of Salai, in Negros. It was a holiday excursion, and the boat was packed with natives out for fun. There was a peddler with a stock of lemon soda-water, sarsaparilla, sticks of boiled rice, cakes, and cigarettes. A game of *monte* was immediately started on the deck, the Filipinos squatting anxiously around the dealer, wagering their *suca ducos* (pennies) or their silver pieces on the turn of certain cards. It was a perfectly good-natured game, rendered absurd by the concentric circles of bare feet surrounding it. There seemed to be a personality about those feet; there were the sleek extremities of some more prosperous councilman or *insurrecto* general; there were the horny feet of the old women, slim and bony, or a pair of great toes quizzically turned in; and there were flat feet, speckled, brown, or yellow, like a starfish cast up on the sand. They seemed to watch the game with interest, and to note every move the dealer made, smiling or frowning as they won or lost. There was a tramway at Salay, drawn by a bull, and driven by a fellow whose chief object seemed to be to linger with the *señorita* at the terminus. The town was hotter than the desert of Sahara, and as sandy; there was little prospect o£ relief save in the distant mountains rising to the clouds in the blue distance.

Returning to our caravansary at Iloilo, we discovered that our beds had been assigned to others; there was nothing left to do but take possession of the first unoccupied beds that we saw. One of our party evidently got into the "Spaniard's" bed, the customary resting-place of the proprietor, for presently we were awakened by the anxious cries of the *muchachos*, *"Señor, señor, el Español viene!"* (Sir, the Spaniard comes!) But he was not to be put out by any Spaniard, and expressed his sentiments by rolling over and emitting a loud snore. The Spaniard, easily excited, on his entrance flew into an awful rage, while the usurper calmly snored, and the *muchachos* peeked in through the door at peril of their lives.

Nothing especially of interest is to be found at Iloilo,—only a long avenue containing Spanish, native, and Chinese stores; a tiny *plaza*, where the city band played and the people promenaded hand in hand; a harbor flecked with white, triangular sails of native *velas*; and the river, where the coasting boats and tugs are lying at the docks. Neat cattle take the place of carabaos here to a great extent. There is the usual stone fort that seems to belong to some scene of a comic opera. America was represented here by a Young Men's Christian Association, a clubhouse, and a *presidente*. The troops then stationed in the town added a certain tone of liveliness.

It was a week of carol-singing in the streets, of comedies performed by strolling bands of children, masses, and concerts in the *plaza*. On Christmas afternoon we went out to the track to see the bicycle races, which at that time were a fad among the Filipinos. The little band played in the grand-stand, and the people cheered the racers as they came laboriously around the turn. The meet was engineered by some American, but, from a standpoint of close finishes, left much to be desired. The market-place on Christmas eve was lighted by a thousand lanterns, and the little people wandered among the booths, smoking their cigarettes and eating peanuts. Until early morning the incessant shuffling in the streets kept up, for every one had gone to midnight mass. Throughout the town the strumming of guitars, the voices of children, and the blare of the brass band was heard, and the next morning Jack-pudding danced on the corner to the infinite amusement of the crowd. As for our own celebration, that was held in the back room of a local restaurant, the Christmas dinner consisting of canned turkey and canned cranberry-sauce, canned vegetables, and ice-cream made of condensed milk.

Chapter V.
On Summer Seas.

The foolish little steamer *Romulus* never exactly knew when she was going, whither away, or where. The cargo being under hatches, all regardless of the advertised time of departure, whether the passengers were notified or not, she would stand clumsily down stream and out to sea. The captain, looking like a pirate in his Tam o'Shanter cap, or the pink little mate with the suggestion of a mustache on his upper lip, if they had been informed about sailing hour, were never willing to divulge the secret. If you tried to argue the matter with them or impress them with a sense of their responsibility; if you attempted to explain the obvious advantages of starting within, say, twenty-four hours of the stated time, they would turn wearily away, irreprehensible, with a protesting gesture.

Not even excepting the Inland Sea, that dreamy waterway among the grottoes, pines, and *torii* of picturesque Japan, there is no sea so beautiful as that around the Southern Philippines. The stately mountains, that go sweeping by in changing shades of green or blue, appeal directly to the imagination. Unpopulated islands—islands of which some curious myths are told of wild white races far in the interior; of spirits haunting mountain-side and vale; volcanoes, in a lowering cloud of sulphurous smoke; narrows, and wave-lashed promontories, where the ships can not cross in the night; great mounds of foliage that tower in silence hardly a stone's throw from the ship, like some wild feature of a dream,—such are the characteristics of the archipelago.

The grandeur of the scenery, the tempered winds, the sense of being alone in an untraveled wilderness, made up in part for the discomforts of the *Romulus*. The tropical sunsets, staining the sky until the whole west was a riot of color, fiery red and gold; the false dawn, and the sunrise breaking the ramparts of dissolving cloud; the moonlight on the waters, where the weird beams make a shimmering path that leads away across the planet waste to *terra incognita*, or to some dank sea-cave where the sirens sing,—this is a day and a night upon the summer seas.

On Summer Seas

At night, as the black prow goes pushing through the phosphorescent waters, porpoises of solid silver, puffing desperately, tumble about the bows, or dive down underneath the rushing hull. The surging waves are billows of white fire. In the electric moonlight the blue mountains, more mysterious than ever, stand out in bold relief. What restless tribes of savages are wandering now through the trackless forests, sleeping in lofty trees, or in some scanty shelter amid the tangled underbrush! The light that flickers in the distant gorge, perchance illumines some religious orgy—some impassioned dance of primitive and pagan men. What spirits are abroad to-night, invoked at savage altars by the incantations of the savage priests—spirits of trees and rivers emanating from the hidden shrines of an almighty one! Or it may be that the light comes from an isolated leper settlement, where the unhappy mortals spend in loneliness their dreary lives.

On the first trip of the *Romulus* I was assigned to a small, mildewed, stuffy cabin, wherethe unsubstantial, watery roaches played at hide-and-seek around the wash-stand and the floor. It was a splendid night to sleep on deck; and so, protected from the stiff breeze by the flapping canvas, on an army cot which the *muchacho* had stretched out, I went to sleep, my thoughts instinctively running into verse:

"The wind was just as steady, and the vessel tumbled more,

But the waves were not as boist'rous as they were the day
before."

It was the rhythm of the sea, the good ship rising on the waves, the
cats'-paws flying into gusts of spray before the driving wind.

I was awakened at four bells by the disturbance of the sailors
swabbing down the deck—an exhibition performance, as the general
condition of the ship led me to think. Breakfast was served down in
the forward cabin, where, with deep-sea appetites, we eagerly
attacked a tiny cup of chocolate, very sweet and thick, a glass of
coffee thinned with condensed milk, crackers, and ladyfingers. That
was all. Some of our fellow-passengers had been there early, as the
dirty table-cloth and dishes testified. A Filipino woman at the further
end was engaged in dressing a baby, while the provincial treasurer,
in his pink pajamas, tried to shave before the dingy looking-glass.
An Indian merchant, a Visayan belle with dirty finger-nails and
ankles, and a Filipino justice of the peace still occupied the table.
Reaching a vacant place over the piles of rolled-up sleeping mats and
camphorwood boxes—the inevitable baggage of the Filipino—I
swept off the crumbs upon the floor, and, after much persuasion,
finally secured a glass of lukewarm coffee and some broken cakes.
The heavy-eyed *muchacho*, who, with such reluctance waited on the
table, had the grimiest feet that I had ever seen.

A second meal was served at ten o'clock, for which the tables were
spread on deck. The plates were stacked up like Chinese pagodas,
and counting them, you could determine accurately the number of
courses on the bill of fare. There were about a dozen courses of fresh
meat and chicken—or the same thing cooked in different styles.
Garlic and peppers were used liberally in the cooking. Heaps of
boiled rice, olives, and sausage that defied the teeth, wrapped up in
tinfoil, "took the taste out of your mouth." Bananas, mangoes,
cheese, and guava-jelly constituted the dessert. After the last plate
had been removed, the grizzled captain at the head of the table
lighted a coarse cigarette, which, in accordance with the Spanish
custom, he then passed to the mate, so that the mate could light his
cigarette. This is a more polite way than to make an offer of a match.
Coffee and cognac was brought on after a considerable interval.

Although this process was repeated course for course at eight o'clock, during the interim you found it was best to bribe the steward and eat an extra meal of crackers.

Our next voyage in the *Romulus* was unpropitious from the start. We were detained five days in quarantine in Manila Bay. There was no breeze, and the hot sun beat down upon the boat all day. To add to our discomforts, there was nothing much to eat. The stock of lady-fingers soon became exhausted, and the stock of crackers, too, showed signs of running out. As an experiment I ordered eggs for breakfast once—but only once. The cook had evidently tried to serve them in disguise, believing that a large amount of cold grease would in some way modify their taste. He did not seem to have the least respect for old age. It was the time of cholera; the boat might have become a pesthouse any moment. But the steward assured us that the drinking water had been neither boiled nor filtered. There was no ice, and no more bottled soda, the remaining bottles being spoken for by the ship's officers. At the breakfast-table two calves and a pig, that had been taken on for fresh meat, insisted upon eating from the plates. The sleepy-eyed *muchacho* was by this time grimier than ever. Even the passengers did not have any opportunity to take a bath. One glance at the ship's bathtub was sufficient.

It was a happy moment when we finally set out for the long rambling voyage to the southern isles. The captain went barefooted as he paced the bridge. A stop at one place in the Camarines gave us a chance to go ashore and buy some bread and canned fruit from the military commissary. How the captain and the mate scowled as we supplemented our elaborate meals with these purchases! One of the passengers, a miner, finally exasperated at the cabin-boy, made an attack upon the luckless fellow, when the steward, who had been wanting an excuse to exploit his authority, came up the hatchway bristling. In his Spanish jargon he explained that he considered it as his prerogative to punish and abuse the luckless boy, which he did very capably at times; that he would tolerate no interference from the passengers. But the big miner only looked him over like a cock-of-the-walk regarding a game bantam. Being a Californian, the miner told the steward in English (which that officer unfortunately did not understand) that if the service did not presently improve, the steward and cabin-boy together would go overboard.

Stopping at Dumaguete, Oriental Negros, where we landed several teachers, with their trunks and furniture, upon the hot sands, most of us went ashore in surf-boats, paddled by the kind of men that figure prominently in the school geographies. It was a chapter from "Swiss Family Robinson,"—the white surf lashing the long yellow beach; the rakish palm-trees bristling in the wind; a Stygian volcano rising above a slope of tropic foliage; the natives gathering around, all open-mouthed with curiosity. At Camaguin, where the boat stopped at the sultry little city of Mambajo, an accident befell our miner. When we found him, he was sleeping peacefully under a *nipa* shade, guarded by a municipal policeman, with the ring of Filipinos clustering around. He had been drinking native *"bino"* (wine), and it had been too much even for him, a discharged soldier and a Californian.

It was almost a pleasant change, the transfer to the tiny launch *Victoria*, that smelled of engine oil and Filipinos, and was commanded by my old friend Dumalagon. The *Victoria* at that time had a most unpleasant habit of lying to all night, and sailing with the early dawn. When I had found an area of deck unoccupied by feet or Filipino babies, Chinamen or ants, I spread an army blanket out and went to sleep in spite of the incessant drizzle which the rotten canopy seemed not to interrupt. I was awakened in the small hours by the rattle of the winch. These little boats make more ado in getting under way than any ocean steamer I have ever known. Becoming conscious of a cloud of opium-smoke escaping from the cockpit, which was occupied by several Chinamen, I shifted to windward, stepping over the sprawling forms of sleepers till I found another place, the only objection to which was the proximity of numerous brown feet and the hot engine-room. The squalling of an infant ushered in the rosy-fingered dawn.

Most of the transportation of the southern islands is accomplished by such boats as the *Victoria*. I can remember well the nights spent on the launch *Da-ling-ding*, an impossible, absurd craft, that rolled from side to side in the most gentle sea. She would start out courageously to cross the bay along the strip of Moro coast in Northern Mindanao; but the throbbing of her engines growing weaker and weaker, she would presently turn back faint-hearted, unable to make headway, at the mercy of a sudden storm, and with the possibility of being swept up on a hostile shore among bloodthirsty and unreasonable Moros. Another time, and we were caught in a typhoon off the north coast. We thought, of course, our little ship was stanch, until we asked the captain his opinion. "If the engines hold out," he replied, "we may come through all right. The engineer says that the old machine will probably blow up now any time, and that the Filipinos have quit working and begun their prayers." Generally a Filipino is the first to give up in a crisis; but I have seen some that managed their canoes in a rough sea with as much skill and coolness as an expert yachtsman could have shown. I have to thank Madroño for the way in which he handled the small boat that put out in a sea like glass and ran into a squall fifteen miles out. All through the morning we had poled along over the crust of coral bottom, where, in the transparent water, indigo fishes swam, where purple starfish sprawled among the coral—coral of many colors and in many forms. But as the wind came up and lashed the choppy sea to whitecaps, as the huge waves swept along and seemed about to knock the little *banca* "off her feet," Madroño, standing on the bamboo outrigger—a framework lashed together with the native cane, the breaking of which would have immediately upset the boat—kept her bow pointed for the shore, although a counter storm threatened to blow us out to the deep sea.

So, after knocking around in *bancas*, picnicking with natives on the chicken-bone and boiled rice; after a wild cruise in the *Thomas*, where the captain and the crew, as drunk as lords, let the old rotten vessel drift, while threatening with a gun the man that dared to meddle with the steering gear; after a dreary six months in a provincial town,—it seemed like coming into a new world to step aboard the clean white transport, with electric-lights and an upholstered smoking-room.

A tourist party, mostly army officers, their wives and daughters, "doing" the archipelago, made up the passenger list of the transport. The officers, now they had settled satisfactorily the question of superiority and "rank," made an agreeable company. There was the Miss Bo Peep, in pink and white, who wore a dozen different military pins, and would not look at any one unless he happened to be "in the service." Like many of the army girls, she had no use for the civilians or volunteers. Her mamma told with pride how, at their last "at home," nobody under the rank of a major had been present. One of the young lieutenants down at Zamboanga, when he found she had not worn his pin, "retired to cry." But then, of course, Bo Peep was not responsible for young lieutenants' hearts. If he had been a captain—well, that is another thing. There was the English sugar-planter from the Tawi-Tawi group, who never lost sight of the ranking officer, who dressed in flannels, changed his clothes three times a day, and who expressed his only ideas to me by virtue of a confidential wink.

For three whole days we were a part of the fresh winds, the tossing waves, the moon and stars. And as the ship plowed through the sea at night, the phosphorescent surge retreated like a line of silver fire.

Chapter VI.
Among the Pagan Tribes.

With Padre Cipriano I had started out on horseback from the little trading station on Davao Bay. We were to strike along the east coast, in the territory of the fierce Mandayas, and to penetrate some distance into the interior in order to convert the pagans with the long eyelashes who inhabited this unknown region. It was a clear day when we set out on our missionary enterprise, and we could see the black peak of Mount Apo, which, according to the legends of the wild Bagobos, is the throne of the great King of Devils, and the gate to hell.

We struck a faint trail leading to the foot-hills where the barren ridges overlooked the sparkling sea—a vast cerulian expanse without a single fleck of a white sail. The trail led through the great fields of buffalo-grass, out of which gigantic solitary trees shot up a hundred feet into the air. There were no signs of life, only the vultures in the topmost branches of the trees. Wild horses, taking flight at our approach, stampeded for the forest. Nothing could be seen in the tall grass. Even in our saddles it was higher than our heads. The trail became more rugged as we entered the big belt of forest on the foot-hills. A wild hog bolted for the jungle with distressed grunts. It was a world of white vines falling from the lofty branches of the trees. The animal life in some of the great trees was wonderful. The branches were divided into zones, wherein each class of bird or reptile had its habitat. Around the base were galleries of white ants. Flying lizards from the gnarled trunk skated through the air. Green reptiles crawled along the horizontal branches. Parrakeets, a colony of saucy green and red balls, screamed and protested from the lower zones. An agile monkey swung from one of the long sweeping vines, and scolded at us from another tree. Bats, owls, and crows inhabited the upper regions, while the buzzards perched like evil omens in the topmost boughs.

Just when our throats were parched from lack of water, we discovered a small mountain torrent gushing over the rocks and bowlders of the rugged slope. Leaning across one of the large bowlders, from a dark pool where the sunlight never penetrated, we scooped up refreshing hatfuls of the ice-cold water. Here was the world as God first found it, when he said that it was good. It was impressive and mysterious. It seemed to wrap us in a mystic spell. What wonder that the pagan tribes that roamed through the interior had peopled it with gods and spirits of the chase, and that the trees and rivers seemed to them the spirits of the good or evil deities? The note of the wood-pigeon sounded on the right. The padre smiled as he looked up. "That is a favorable omen," he declared. "In the religion of the river-dwellers, the Bagobos, when the wood-dove calls, it is the voice of God. Hark! It is coming from the right. It is a favorable sign, and we can go upon our journey undisturbed. But had we heard it on the left, it would have been to us a warning to turn back. Our journey then would have been unpropitious, and we would have been afraid to go on farther."

"Does it not seem like a grand cathedral," said the padre, "this vast forest? In the days when Northern Europe was a wilderness and savage people hunted in the forests; in the days when the undaunted Norsemen braved the stormy ocean in their daring craft,—here, in these woods, the petty chiefs and head men held their courts of justice after the traditions of their tribes, just as they do to-day. Here they have set their traps—the arrows loosened from a bamboo spring—and while they waited, they have left the offering of eggs and rice for the good deity. Here they have hunted their blood enemies, lying in ambush, or digging pitfalls where the sharpened stakes were planted. Tama, the god of venery, has lured the deer into their traps; Tumanghob, god of harvest, whom they have invited to their feasts, has made the corn and the *camotes* prosper; Mansilitan, the great spirit, has descended from the mountain-tops and aided them against their enemies."

We knew that it was growing late by the deep shadows of the woods. So, taking our bearings with a pocket compass, we turned east in the direction of the coast. There was no trail to follow, and we blundered on as best we could. We had now been in the saddle for ten hours. The ponies stumbled frequently, for they were almost spent. The moon rose, and the hoary mountain loomed up just ahead of us. "We seem to be lost," said the padre; "that is a strange peak to me." But nevertheless we kept on toward the east. Soon we had passed beyond the forest, which appeared behind us a great dusky belt. The numerous rocks and crags made progress difficult, almost impossible.

"Look!" said the padre, "do you see that light?" We tethered the ponies at a distance, crept up stealthily behind the rocks, and reconnoitered. And what we looked on was the strangest sight that ever mortal eyes beheld. It was like living again in the Dark Ages— in the days before the sages and the sun-myth. It was like turning back the leaves of history—back to the legendary, prehistoric times.

A lofty grove encircled a chaotic mass of rock. The clearing was illuminated by the flaring torches carried by a dusky band of men. Weird shadows leaped and played in the dense foliage, where, high above the ground, rude shelters had been made in the thick branches of the trees. The form of a woman, flashing with silver trinkets when the rays of light fell on her, was descending from a tree by means of a long parasitic vine. Around the palm-leaf huts that occupied the center of the amphitheater, an altar of bamboo had been erected. We could see, in the dim light, rude images of idols standing in front of every hut and near the altar.

As our eyes became accustomed to the gloom, we could make out the forms of men and women, dressed in brilliant colors and with silver bracelets on their arms. In silence we crept closer. The crowd was visibly excited. It was evident that something of a solemn and extraordinary nature was about to be performed. There were the chief assassins, so the padre whispered to me, who were decorated savagely, according to the number of victims each had slain. The ordinary men wore open vests or jackets and loose pantaloons. The women, evidently decked out with a complement of finery in honor of the celebration, wore short aprons reaching to the knee. Some wore gold collars around their necks and silver-embroidered slippers on their feet. Their bare arms sparkled with the coils of silver bands and bracelets that encircled them, while silver anklets jingled with the movement of their feet. They had red tassels in their hair, and earrings made of pieces of carved bone. A number of dancing-girls, as they appeared to be, had strings of red and yellow beads or animals' teeth fastened around their necks. Their breasts were covered with short bodices that fell so as to leave a portion of the waist exposed.

The chief assassins were completely clad in scarlet, indicating that the wearer had disposed of more than twenty enemies. The lesser assassins wore yellow handkerchiefs around their heads, and some were dignified with scarlet vests. A miserable naked slave was pinioned where he had been thrown upon the ground near by. Although of the inferior race of the Bilanes from Lake Buluan, his eyes flashed as he regarded the assembled people scornfully. They were to offer up a human sacrifice to Mansilitan, the all-powerful god.

The head men seemed to be engaged in a dispute. A wild hog, also lying near the altar, was the object of their serious attention. After they had chattered for a while, and having evidently decided on the pig, the drums and tambourines struck up a doleful melody, and those assembled joined in a solemn chant. The pig was carefully lifted to the altar, and the chant grew more intensified. A number of dancing-girls, describing mystic circles with their jeweled arms, were trembling violently, bending rhythmically, gracefully from side to side. The music seemed to hypnotize the people, who kept shuffling with their feet monotonously on the ground. The leader of the dance then stuck the living pig with a sharp dagger. As the red blood spurted out, she caught a mouthful of it, and applying her mouth quickly to the wound, she sucked the fluid till she reeled and fell away. Another followed her example, and another, till the pig was drained.

It was not difficult to fancy a like orgy with the quivering slave upon the altar in the place of the wild hog. The spirit of Mansilitan then came down—the spirit was, of course, invisible—and talked with the head men about their enemies, the crops, and game. The chiefs were chewing cinnamon and betel till their mouths were red. The master of ceremonies then brought out enormous quantities of *tuba*, and his guests completed the religious ceremony with a wholesale drunk.

Under the cover of the darkness, Padre Cipriano and I slipped away. We shuddered at what we had just seen, and were silent. Leading the ponies a short distance into the brush, we slept upon the blankets which the ponies had completely saturated with their perspiration. All night we dreamed of human sacrifices and the warm blood spurting from the victim's breast.... They had the padre now upon the altar, and the chief had bidden me to take the knife and draw his blood. But the great god—a creature with the horns of a bull carabao—descended, crying that the enemy was now upon us and the crops had failed. From our uneasy sleep the crowing of the jungle-fowl awakened us, and for the first time we expressed ourselves in words. "Padre," I said, "it's just like being in a book of Du Chaillu's or Rider Haggard's;" and the padre smiled.

After the ponies, who were very stiff, were limbered up a bit, we traveled on in the direction of the sea. We stopped beside a mountain stream to bathe and eat a breakfast of canned sausages. That afternoon we rode into a small Mandaya settlement where the head man showed Padre Cipriano every courtesy at his command. They listened eagerly to Padre Cipriano, who could speak their language well, as he explained to them about another Mansilitan, greatest God of all. A number of them even consented to be baptized; but I am very much afraid that the conversion was at best a transient one. The head man ordered that his runners bring into the village of Davao for the padre gifts of game, wild hog, deer, and jungle-fowl, and, after the padre had presented him with several strings of green and yellow beads—for the Mandayas have no use for black beads as their neighbors, the Manobos have—we took our departure, guided to the trail by a distinguished warrior.

During our sojourn in the settlement we picked up many curious and interesting facts. Like most of the wild tribes of Mindanao, that of the Mandayas is athletic and robust. The faces of the men are somewhat girlish and effeminate, while the expressions of the warriors are unique. Upon their countenances cunning, cruelty, and diabolical resource are stamped indelibly. In front of every house a wooden idol stands, while inside, on a little table, is a smaller image overwhelmed by gifts of fruit and rice, which members of the family continually leave upon the shrine. A tiny sack of rice hangs from the idol's neck, and betel-nuts for him to chew are placed where they are easily accessible. During the preparation of the evening meal, one of the family will play upon a native instrument, dancing meanwhile around the room, and lifting up his voice in supplication to the deity.

The petty ruler or head man is chosen by a natural process of selection. He is invariably one who, by his prowess and intelligence, commands the respect and the obedience of all. Assisted by a local justice of the peace, a bailiff, and a secretary, he conducts affairs according to the old traditions handed down almost from the beginning of the world. The families live together, thus preserving clans, while blood feuds with the neighboring clans or tribes lead to a system of perpetual extermination, which will be continued till the tribe becomes extinct. And if the enemy himself can not be killed, the nearest relative or friend will satisfy the aggressor's hatred just as well. Cannibalism has been practiced in this tribe with fearful and disgusting rites. The human sacrifices that they make appease not only the great spirit, but the lesser ones, the man and wife, or evil spirits, and the father and son, good spirits. When they go to war, the lighting men use lances, swords, and bows and arrows. On their wooden shields, daubed over with red paint, arranged around the edges like a fringe, are tufts of hair—the souvenirs of men whom they have killed. Their coats of mail are made of carabao horn cut into small plates, or of pieces of rattan.

The only use they have for money is to make it into decorations and embellishments for their most valued weapons, anklets and rings and collars, which they wear without discrimination. They are a very imaginative and a superstitious people. From their infancy they are familiar with the dwarfs, the giants, and the witches, which, according to the tales of the old women, haunt the woods. A crocodile that lives down in the center of the earth causes the earthquakes, and, to put a stop to these, the crocodiles must be persuaded by religious incantations to go back to bed. A solar eclipse threatens a great calamity to them, and they are sure that if they do not frighten away the serpent who is trying to devour the sun, their land will never see the morning light again. To this end they unite in beating drums and making a loud noise with sticks.

They bury their dead in coffins made of hollowed logs. A pot of rice and the familiar weapons will be placed within the grave, so that the soul will have protection and a food supply for the long journey. And, like Jacob, the prospective bridegroom has to serve the parents of the bride for five or seven years before the marriage ceremony can take place. The marriage-ties are sacred even with this savage race. The groom-to-be, making from time to time, gifts of wild hogs, rice, and weapons to the parents of the bride-elect, is finally rewarded with the bride, and with a dowry as well; perhaps a slave, a bucket of *tuba*, or a silver-mounted bolo. The average value of a bride is five or six slaves, which the bridegroom pays if he is able. At the marriage ceremony the contracting parties generally present each other with small cups of rice, to signify that they must now endeavor mutually to support each other.

Among other tribes of the interior of Mindanao, in the river basins of the Salug and the Agusan, along the east coast, and Davao Bay, and on the mountain slopes, are the Manobos, possibly of Indonesian origin, kings of the wilderness, inhabiting the river valleys; the intrepid Attas, from the slopes of the volcano Apo; the Bagobos, with their interesting faces and bright clothes, living to the east of Apo; the fierce Dulaganes of the forests, whom the Moros fear; Samales, from the island in Davao Bay, strong, bearded people, with big hands and feet; Bilanes, from Lake Buluan, a wandering, nomadic race; and the Monteses of the north, sun-worshipers and petty traders.

All of these tribes are probably of Indonesian origin, an independent origin from that of the Visayans, the Tagalogs, the Negritos, or the Moros, but of the same social level with the Malay-Chinese pagans of the northern isles.

I used to see the Montese traders in the market-place of Cagayan (Misamis), their mobile mouths swimming with betel-juice, with rings and bracelets on their toes and arms, the girls with hair banged saucily, adorned with bells and tassels, and with bodices inadequately covering the breasts; and as they squatted down on the woven mats, around the honey or the wax they had for sale, they looked like gypsies from Roumania or Hungary. The men wore bright, tight-fitting pantaloons and dirty turbans. They resemble the Moros somewhat in appearance, and have either intermingled with this tribe or else can trace their origin to Borneo. While they are not so wild or so exclusive as their fellow-tribes, they quickly resent intrusion into their towns or their society.

They carry on a slave trade with their neighbors, stealing or kidnaping from the other tribes, and being stolen from in turn. The women of some tribes brand their children, filling in the wound with a blue dye, that serves as an identification if they happen to be snatched away. The various religious ideas of these pagans are intangible and indeterminate. The forest seems to be the abiding-place of gods. Some tribes will offer feasts to these divinities, either leaving the flesh and rice out in the woods to find that it has disappeared next morning, or, in many cases, eating it themselves, provided that the god, who has been earnestly invited, fails to come. The god of disease is also recognized, and natives living on the coast have been known, in the time of cholera, to fill canoes with rice and fruit in order to appease this deity, and leave the boats to drift out with the tide.

Among the Bagobos, curious traditions and religious rites exist. Every Bagobo thinks he has two souls or spirits; one a good one, and the other altogether to the bad. To them the summit of Mount Apo is the throne of the great Devil King, who watches over the crater with his wife. The crater is the entry-way to hell, and no one can ascend the mountain if he has not previously offered up a human sacrifice, so that the Devil King may have a taste of human flesh and blood, and being satiated, will desire no more. Cannibalism has existed in these regions more as a religious orgy than a means of sustenance. A dish was made consisting of the quivering vitals of the victim, mixed with sweet potatoes, rice, or fruit.

Upon the death of any member of the tribe the house in which he lived is burned. The body is placed within a hollow tree, and stands for several days, while a barbaric feast is held around it. The Samales bury their dead upon a coral island, placing them in grottoes, which they visit annually with harvest offerings.

Chapter VII.
A Lost Tribe and the Servants of Mohammed.

Wandering, always wandering through the mountains and forests since the years began,—destined to wander till the forests fall.

Throughout the archipelago, in the dense mountain woods, sleeping in trees or on the ground, straying away in search of game, without a fixed place of abode, live the Negritos, aborigines, the pigmy vagrants of the Philippines. These little men, molesting no one, yet considering the rest of mankind as their enemy, and wishing only to be left alone, have hidden in the unexplored interior. Where they have come from is a mystery. It might have been that, in the ages past, the chain of islands from Luzon to Borneo was a part of Asia, an extensive mountain system populated by the tiny men found there to-day. If so, then they were driven to the highlands by the cataclysm that in prehistoric ages might have broken up the mainland into islands, leaving only the summits of the mountains visible.

Or otherwise, might not these wanderers, who have their prototypes among the pigmies of dark Africa, or in the dwarfs inhabiting New Guinea—might they not have set sail from Caffraria, New Guinea, or the country of the Papuans, long years before the Christian era, like the "Jumblies," in their frail canoes, perhaps escaping persecution, driven by the winds and currents, to land at last on the unpeopled shores of Filipinia?

In time came the Malayans of low culture, now the pagan tribes of the interior, and a conflict—primitive men fighting with rude weapons, clubs, and stones—ensued for the possession of the coast. In that event the smaller men were driven back into the territory that they occupy to-day. The races intermingled, and a medley of strange, mongrel tribes resulted. They have wandered, scattering themselves abroad about the islands. Influenced by various environment, each tribe adopted different customs and built up from common roots the different dialects. These tribes have always been, and always will be, mere barbarians and savages. In the pure type of Negritos, spindle legs, large turned-in feet, weak bodies, and large heads are noticeable. Shifting eyes, flat noses, kinky hair, and teeth irregularly set,—these are Negrito characteristics, though they frequently occur in the *mestizo* types. The Igorrotes of Luzon, whose ancestors were possibly the aborigines and the worst element of the invaders, are to-day the cannibals and the head-hunters of the north. In Abra, province of Luzon, the Burics and their neighbors, the Busaos, both of a Negrito-Malay origin, use poisoned darts, tattoo their bodies, and adorn themselves with copper rings and caps of rattan decorated with bright feathers. The Manguianes, of the mountains of Mindoro, dress in rattan coils, supplemented with a scanty apron.

These Malayan races were, in their turn, driven back by later Malays, who became the nucleus of the Tagalog, Bicol, Ilocano, and Visayan races, taking possession of the coast and mouths of rivers, and governing themselves, or being governed by hereditary rajas, just as when, three centuries ago, Magellan and Legaspi found them. The Moros, or Mohammedan invaders, were first heard from when, in 1597, Spain first tried to organize them into a dependent government. These treacherous pirates, the descendants of the fierce Dyacs of Borneo, had begun still earlier to terrorize the southern coasts, raiding the villages and carrying off the children into slavery. In 1599 a Moro fleet descended on the coast of Negros and Panay, and would, no doubt, have occupied this territory permanently had not the arms of Spain been there to interfere. Hereafter Spanish galleons were to oppose the progress of these pirate fleets, while troops of infantry were to defeat the savages on land. The Spaniards early in the seventeenth century succeeded in establishing a foothold on the island of Jolo and at Zamboanga. It was Father Malchior de Vera who designed the fort at Zamboanga, which was destined to become the scene of many an attack by Moro warriors, and to be the base of military operations against the surrounding tribes. A Jesuit mission was established in the sultan's territory after the defeat of the Mohammedans by Corcuera. In the interior, around the shores of Lake Lanao, the fighting padre, Friar Pedro de San Augustin, backing the cross with Spanish infantry, carried the Christian war into the country of the infidels, continuing the conflict that for many years had made a battleground of Spain. It was in memory of their old enemies, the Moors, that when the Spaniards met the infidels in eastern lands, they named them Moros (Moors).

Negrito Pigmy Vagrants

The war between Spain and the Moros was relentless. Time and again the pirates had been punished by the Spanish admirals, until, in 1725, the sultan sent a Chinese envoy to Manila to negotiate a truce. A treaty was ratified, but broken, and again the Sulu Moros learned what Spanish hell was like. In spite of this continual warfare the Mohammedans grew stronger, and in 1754 the ocean was infested with the Moro *vintas*, till another friar, Father Ducos, in a sea-fight off the coast of Northern Mindanao, sunk one hundred and fifty of their boats and killed three thousand men. Bantilan, the usurper of the Sulu throne, was one of the foremost of the mischief-makers who, in 1767, sent a pirate fleet as far north as Manila Bay. Although the Spaniards had repeatedly won victories in Jolo, Zamboanga, and Davao, and by treaties had made all this country vassal to the crown of Spain, up to the time of the evacuation of the Philippines, when, as a last act, they had sent their own tiny gunboats to the bottom of Lanao, they never had become the undisputed masters of the territory.

One of the pleasantest friends I had while I was in the Islands was Herr Altman, an orchid collector, who had risked his life a hundred times among the savages of the interior in the pursuance of the passion of his life. "One afternoon," he said, "when we were in the forests of Luzon, my native guides approached me with broad grins. I thought, perhaps, they had discovered some new orchid; so I followed them. But I was unprepared for what they were about to show me. Since then I have had much experience among the wild tribes, but at this time everything was new to me. They motioned silence as, with broadening grins, they now approached what seemed to be a clearing in the woods. I could not think why they should be amused; but they are very easily delighted, just like children, and I thought that it would do no harm to humor them. Then I was startled by the howling of a dog and a strange sound coming through the woods.

Still following my guides, I brought up in a growth of underbrush on a small precipice that overlooked an open space among the trees. Looking in the direction in which they pointed, I beheld a group of tiny black men dancing in a circle around what seemed to be a section of a fallen tree. Off to the side, the women, slightly smaller than the men, were cooking a wild hog on a spit, over a smoking fire. Their hair was thick and woolly and uncombed. Their arms and ankles were adorned with copper bracelets. Some of the men wore leather thongs that dangled from their legs. There were a few rude shelters in the clearing, merely improvised affairs of branches. As the men danced they sent up a song in a high, piping voice, and several hungry dogs, who had been watching enviously the roasting meat, howled sympathetically and in unison. It finally occurred to me that we were the spectators of a funeral ceremony; that the section of a tree was nothing less than the rough coffin of the dead Negrito. We continued to watch them for a time, while, having finished dancing, they began their feast. The only dishes that they had were cocoanut-shells, out of which they drank immoderate amounts of *tuba*. The funeral ceremony, as I understand it, lasts for several days—as long as the supply of meat and *tuba* lasts. The coffin, which appeared to me a hollowed log, is but a section of a certain bark sealed up at either end with wax. The burial is made under the house in the case of those tribes living near the coast; or in a stockade, which protects the body against desecration from the enemy."

It was with feelings such as one might entertain when looking at a mermaid or an inhabitant of Mars, that I first saw a genuine Negrito in a prison at Manila. The wretched pigmy had been brought in to the city from his inaccessible retreat in the great forest; he was dazed and frightened at the white men and the things they did. He was a miserable little fellow, with distrustful eyes, and twisted legs, and pigeon toes. He died after a few days of captivity, during which time he had not spoken. A dumb obedience marked his relations with the guard. The white man's civilization was as disagreeable and unnatural to him as his nomadic life would be to us. A fish could just as well live out of water as this pigmy in the white man's land.

A few of the Negritos near the coast, however, have been touched by civilizing influences. They inhabit towns of small huts built on poles, which they abandon on the death of any one within. The house wherein a death occurs is generally burned. They plant a little corn and rice, but often move away before the crop is harvested. They are too lazy to raise anything; too weak to capture slaves. During the heavy rains, when the great woods are saturated, they protect themselves against the cold by wrapping blankets around their bodies. At night they often share the tree with birds and monkeys, sheltered from rain and dampness by the canopy of foliage. They have a head man for their villages—sometimes a member of another tribe, who, on account of his superior attainments, holds the respect of all. They hunt with bows and arrows; weapons which, by means of constant use, they handle with dexterity. At night their villages are located through the incessant barking of the hungry dogs, which always follow them around. Sleeping in huts, in order to prevent mosquitoes from annoying them, they often build a fire beneath them, toasting themselves until their flesh becomes a crust of scales.

In the south Camarines, and in Negros, they will often come down to the coast towns, trading the wax and sweet potatoes of the mountains for sufficient rice to last them several days. They sometimes work a day or two in the adjacent hemp or rice fields, receiving for their labor a small measure of the rice. When they have eaten this, they fast until their hunger drives them down to work again. Their marriage relations are peculiar. While the father of the family has but one true wife, a number of women are dependent on him, widows or relatives who have attached themselves to him. The children receive their names from rivers, animals, or trees. If they were taken out of their environment when very young they might be educated, as experiments have shown that the Negrito children have the same impulses of generosity, the same attachment to their friends, the same joys, sorrows, and sensations, that belong to children everywhere. Only their little souls are lost forever in the wilderness.

Neither the pagan tribes nor the Negritos read or write. The Moros, too, are very ignorant, only the priests and students being able to read passages from the Koran and make the Arabic characters. The latest Malay immigrants, who had been influenced by Indian culture, introduced a style of writing that is very queer. Three vowels were used,—a, e, and u. The consonants were represented by as many signs that look a good deal like our shorthand. Although there were three characters to represent the vowels when used alone, whenever a consonant would be pronounced with "a," only the sign of the consonant was used. In order to express a final consonant, or one without the vowel, a tiny cross was made below the character. If "e" was wanted, a dot would be placed over the letter that expressed the consonant, or if the vowel was to be "u," the dot was placed below.

Some rainy day, when you have nothing else to do, you can invent some characters to represent our consonants, and with the aid of dots and crosses, write a letter to yourself, and see how you would get along if you were forced to use that kind of alphabet at school. The natives use the Spanish alphabet to-day, which is much like our own. Their language, being full of particles, sounds very funny when they talk. All you would understand would be perhaps, pag, naga, naca, mag, tag, paga; and all this would probably convey but little meaning to you. It is a curious fact that while the dialects of all the tribes are different, many of the ordinary words are common, being slightly changed in the transition. The language is of a Malayan origin, but has a number of Sanskrit words as well as Arabic. From studying these dialects, comparing the construction of the sentence as expressed by different tribes, and by comparing the inflections of homogeneous verbs and nouns, one might arrive at the conclusion that these tribes and races, differing so strikingly among each other, mutually antagonistic, all belong to one great family and have a common origin. But that is a question for the anthropologists to settle; one that will give even the professors all the trouble that they want, and make them wrinkle up their learned foreheads, while among them they arrive at widely-varying decisions, which will be as mutually exclusive as the tribes themselves.

It was a rainy day in the dense woods along the Iligan-Marahui road. The soft ground oozed beneath the feet, and a continual dripping was kept up from the low-hanging, saturated foliage. The Moro interpreter, in a red-striped suit and prominent gilt buttons, had come into camp with the report that one of the dattos at Malumbung wanted the military doctor to come up and treat his child, who was afflicted with a fever. The datto had offered protection for the "medico," and, as a fee, a bottle of pure gold. The guides and soldiers, who were waiting in the forest, would conduct the doctor to Malumbung if he cared to go.

"This sounds like a pretty good adventure," said the commanding officer to me. "How would you like to go along?" The doctor had accepted the offer of the Moros, and he now reiterated the commanding officer's invitation. "It's going to be a rather long, stiff hike," he said. "We'll have to sleep to-night out in the woods, and there's no telling whether the Moros mean good faith or not. Remember that, in case the child should die while I am there, the Moros will believe that I have killed it, and will probably make matters more or less unpleasant for us both. I operated once upon a fellow over in Tagaloan who died under the knife. As soon as the spectators saw that he was hardly due to come to life again, they crowded around me with their bolos drawn, and if a friend of mine among them had not interfered, I would have followed my subject very speedily."

It was arranged that we take with us a small squad of regulars to carry the provisions and go armed, "in case there should be any game upon the way." As this arrangement seemed to satisfy the Moros, though it did not please them much, we started, covering the first half mile along the clayey road through driving rain, and turning off into the Moro trail around the summit of the hill. The Moros led the way with their peculiar lurching stride that covered a surprising distance in a very short time. Soon we were in the heart of the vast wilderness. We passed by colonies of monkeys, who severely reprimanded us from their secure retreat among the tree-tops. One of the soldiers killed a python with his Krag—a swollen creature, that could hardly be distinguished from the overhanging vines—that measured twenty feet from head to tail. The Moros silently unslipped their knives, and dextrously removed the skin. We camped that night in shelter tents, although the ground was soaked, and a cold breath penetrated the damp woods. All night the jungle-fowl and monkeys kept up an incessant obligato, and the forest seemed to re-echo with mysterious and far-off sounds. At daylight we pushed on, and late in the afternoon arrived at the small Moro settlement. The tiny *nipa* houses, set up on bamboo poles, were rather a poor substitute for shelter; but on reaching them after our two days in the forest, it was like arriving in a civilized community. The doctor went immediately to the datto's house, a large one with a steep roof, where he dosed the infant with a little quinine.

There were about five hundred Moros in the village under the datto, who ruled absolutely as by hereditary right. While he, of course, was feudal to the nearest sultan, in his own community he was a lord and prince. Most of the people were his slaves and fighting men. His private warriors, or his bodyguard, were armed with krisses, *campalans*, and spears, with shields of carabao hide, and coats of mail of buffalo-horn, as defensive armor. The favorite weapons of the datto were elaborately inlaid with the ivory cut from the tusks of the wild boar. His dress was also distinctive, and when new must have been very brilliant. It was fastened with pearl buttons, while along the outside seams of his tight pantaloons a row of smaller buttons ran. A dirty silk handkerchief wound around his head, the corner overlapping on the side, made an appropriate and fitting headgear. He had several wives, for whom he had paid in all a sum amounting to a hundred sacks of rice and twenty cattle. He had lost considerably on his speculations, having divorced three wives and being unable to secure a rebate on the price that he had paid for them.

As soon as the doctor had completed his attentions to the patient, the *pandita* (priest) appeared, and asked him to account for the strange happenings that had occurred in the community. The village was in a state of panic, and unless a stop were put to the proceedings soon, there was no telling what the end might be. It seemed that during the night a number of children had been murdered secretly. Their mutilated bodies had been left at morning at the gates of their respective dwellings. These murders had been going on for several days, and though the houses had been guarded by a man armed with a *campilan* at night, the children would be mysteriously missing in the morning. It was evidently, said the priest, the work of devils. A big hand had been seen to snatch one of the children from its parent's arms; and under the houses of those afflicted could be seen a weird fire glowing in the dead of night.

The people claimed the murderer was none else than the big man of the woods, whose footprints, like the impressions of a cocoanut-shell, had been discovered in the soft ground near the border of the forest. There was a crazy prophet living in a tree, and he had seen the wife of the big man, half black, half white, wandering near the territory of the lake. The prophet had also seen a star fall from the sky, and he had followed it to see where it had struck the earth. He found there a huge stone, which, as he looked upon it, changed to a wild hog. Then the wild hog had vanished, and a flock of birds had risen from the ground. In place of the rock, a stone hand now appeared, and breaking off a finger of it, the prophet had discovered that, when burnt, its fumes had power to put the whole community to sleep. In this way had the big man of the woods been able to defy the guards and to assassinate the children at his will.

The doctor, thinking that these deeds had been performed by somebody impelled by lust—the lust of seeing blood and quivering flesh—determined to investigate. Suspicion pointed to the crazy prophet, and the guards directed us to his impossible abode. The prophet was accused directly of the crime, and, being convinced that he was found out by the white man's magic, he confessed. The datto sentenced him to be beheaded, and seemed disappointed when we would not stay to see this operation. He even offered to turn the victim loose among the crowd, and let them strike him down with krisses. Had we desired, we could have had the places of honor in the line, and used the datto's finest weapons. The people, he said, were puzzled at our lack of interest, for the occasion would have been a sort of festival for them. But seeing that we were obdurate, the datto served our farewell meal—baked jungle-fowl and rice— and, after offering to purchase our Krag-Jorgesens at an attractive price, he bade us all good-bye.

On the way back, our guides surprised us by their climbing and swimming. There was one place where the Agus River had been spanned by jointed bamboo poles; while we crossed like funambulists, depending for our balance on a slender rail, the Moros leaped into the rushing torrent, near the rapids, swimming like rats against the stream, and reaching the other side ahead of us. One of the guides went up a tall macao-tree, pulling himself up by the long parasitic vines, and bracing himself against the tree-trunk with his feet, to get an orchid that was growing high among the foliage. Though we expressed our admiration at these feats, the guides preserved their customary proud demeanor, and refused to be moved by applause.

Their active life in the vast wilderness has given them athletic, supple bodies, which they handle to a nicety when fighting. Although the Moros build stone forts and mount them with old-fashioned cannon; although their arsenals are fairly well supplied with Remingtons and Mausers, their warriors generally prefer to fight with bolos. These weapons never leave their side. They sleep with them, and they are buried with them. Their heavy *campalans* are fastened to their hands by thongs, so that, in case the hand should slip, the warrior would not fall without his knife. The Moros in a hand-to-hand fight are extremely agile. Holding the shield on the left arm, they flourish the bolo with their right, dodging, leaping, and jeering at the antagonist in order to disconcert or frighten him.

While their religion and fanaticism render them almost foolhardy in a battle, if a Moro sees that he is beaten and that escape is possible, he will avail himself of opportunities to fight another day. If brought to bay, however, he is desperate, and in his more religious moments he will throw himself on a superior enemy, expecting a sure death, but confident of riding the white horse to paradise if he succeeds in spilling the blood of infidels.

Although distrustful, lazy, and malignant, the Moro is consistent in his hatred for the unbeliever, and untiring on the war-path. Scorning all manner of work, he leads an active forest life, killing the wild pig, which religious scruples prevent his eating, and waging war against the neighboring tribes. He is a born slave-catcher and a pirate. He will drink sea-water when no other is available. He shows a diabolical cunning in the manufacture of his weapons. Nothing can be more terrible than the long, snaky blade of a Malay kriss. The harpoons, with which he spears the hogs, come apart at a slight pull. The point of the spear on catching in the flesh holds fast. The handle, however, becoming detached, though held to the barbed point by a thong, catches and holds the hog fast in the underbrush. The head-ax is a long blade turned at just the proper angle to decapitate the victim scientifically.

Ignorant and perfectly indifferent to the observations that their creed prescribes, the Moros gather at the rude mosque to the beating of a monstrous drum. Seated around upon straw mats, they chatter and chew betel-nut while the *pandita* reads a passage from a manuscript copy of the Koran. These copies are guarded sacredly, and only the young men who are studying for the priesthood are instructed from them. The priests of the first class are able to read and write, and it is better to have made the pilgrimage to Mecca. The birth of Mohammed is celebrated by a feast at harvest-time. Another occasion for a feast is given by the marriage ceremony. Bridegrooms are encouraged to provide these banquets by the administration of a beating if delinquent, or in case the food provided fails to meet the expectations of the guests. On the completion of this function, the bridegroom bathes his feet; then chewing *buya*, seated on a mat beside the bride, his hand and hers are covered by a napkin while the priest goes through the proper gestures and recites a verse from the Koran. The wedding celebration then degenerates into a drunken dance.

The bodies of the dead are wrapped in a white shroud, and buried in a crescent trench, together with enough meat, fruit, and water to sustain the spirit on its trip to paradise. The priest, before departing, eats a meal of buffalo-meat or other game above the grave. The grave is then turned over to a guard of soldiers, who remain there for a few days, or as long as they are paid.

Though the Americans have tried to deal in good faith with these fanatics, little has been accomplished either in the way of civilizing them or pacifying them. The Moro schools at Jolo and at Zamboanga have been failures. Teachers of manual training have been introduced to no avail. The Moro could be no more treacherous if his ancestors had sprung from tigers' wombs. A Moro boy, employed for years by one of my American acquaintances at Iligan, rewarded his master recently by cutting his throat at night. As superstitious as he is fanatic and uncivilized, the Moro is a failure as a member of the human race. Even the children are the incarnation of the fiend. There was that boy at Iligan who worked at the officer's club, and who hung over the roulette-wheel like a perfect devil, crowing with demoniac glee when he was lucky. These are our latest citizens—this batch of serpents' eggs hatched out in human form; and those who have seen the Moro in his native home will tell you that, whatever his latent possibilities may be, he can not yet be dealt with as a man.

Our Latest Citizens

Chapter VIII.
In a Visayan Village.

The fountain on the corner, where the brown, barefooted girls with bamboo water-tubes would gather at the noon hour and at supper-time, was shaded in the heat of the day by a mimosa-tree. The *Calle de la Paz y Buen Viaje* (Street of Peace and a Good Journey), flanked by sentinel-like bonga-trees and hedged in by a bamboo fence, stretches away through the banana-groves toward the fantastic mountains. A puffing carabao comes down the long street, dragging the heavy stalks of newly-cut bamboo. The pig that has been rooting in the grass, looks up, and, seeing what is coming, bolts with staccato grunts unceremoniously through the bamboo fence.

In the little drygoods-store across the street, Felicidad, the dusky-eyed proprietress, has gone to sleep while waiting for a customer. She has discarded her *chinelas* and her *piña* yoke. Her brown arms resting on the table pillow her unconscious head. Her listless fingers clasp a half-smoked cigarette.

The stock of *La Aurora* is a comprehensive one, including printed cotton goods from China, red and green belts with nickel fastenings, uncomfortable-looking Spanish shoes, a bottle of quinine sulphate tablets, an assortment of perfumery and jewelry, rosaries and crucifixes, towels and handkerchiefs, and dainty *piña* fabrics. The arrival of the *Americano* is the signal for the neighbors and the neighbors' children, having nothing in particular to do, to flock around. The Filipino curiosity again!

On the next corner, where the wooden Atlas braces up the balcony, the *Chino* store is sheltered from the sun by curtains of alternate blue and white. Here *Chino* Santiago, in his cool pajamas, audits the accounts with the assistance of the wooden counting frame, while *Chino* José, his partner, with his paintbrush stuck behind his ear, is following the ledger with his long, curved finger-nail. Both *Chinos*, being Catholics, have taken native wives, material considerations having influenced the choice; but *Maestro* Pepin says that, nevertheless, they are unpopular because they work too hard and cause the fluctuations in the prices. By pursuing a consistent system of abstractions from the rice-bags, by an innocent adulteration of the *tinto* wine, these two *comerciantes* have acquired considerable wealth.

The bland proprietor will greet you with a smile, and offer you the customary cigarette. And if the prices quoted are unsatisfactory, they are at least elastic and are easily adjusted for a personal friend. Along the shelf the opium-scented line of drygoods is available, while portraits of the saints and *Neustra Señorita del Rosario*, whose conical skirt conceals the little children of the Church, hang from the wall. Suspended from the ceiling are innumerable hanging lamps with green tin shades. A line of fancy handkerchiefs, with Dewey's portrait and the Stars and Stripes embroidered in the corners, is displayed on wires stretched overhead across the store. Bolo blades, chocolate-boilers, rice-pots, water-jars, and crazy looking-glasses are disposed around, while in the glass case almost anything from a bone collar-button to a musical clock is likely to be found. Santiago would be glad to have you open an account here and, unlike the Filipino, he will never trouble you about your bill.

The market street is lined with *nipa* booths, where *señoritas* play at keeping shop, presiding over the army of unattractive articles exposed for sale. Upon a rack the cans of salmon are drawn up in a battalion, a detachment of ex-whisky bottles filled with kerosene or *tanduay*, bringing up the rear. Certain stock articles may be invariably found at these *tiendas*,—boxes of matches, balls of cotton thread, bananas, *buya*, eggs and cigarettes, and the inevitable brimming glass of *tuba*, stained a dark-red color from the frequent applications of the betel-chewing mouth.

Although the stream of commerce flows in a small way where the almighty *'suca duco* is the medium of exchange, gossip is circulated freely; for without the telegraph or telephone, news travels fast in Filipinia. The withered hag, her scanty raiment scarcely covering her bony limbs, squatting upon the counter in the midst of *guinimos*, bananas, and dried fish, and spitting a red pool of betel-juice, will chatter the day long with the *señora* in the booth across the street. The purchaser should not feel delicate at seeing her bare feet in contact with the spiced bread that he means to buy, nor at the swarms of flies around the reeking mound of *guinimos* scraped up in dirty wooden bowls, and left in the direct rays of the sun.

Dogs, pigs, chickens, and children tumble in the dust. Dejected Filipino ponies, tethered to the shacks, are waiting for their masters to exhaust the *tuba* market. Down the lane a panting carabao, with a whole family clinging to its back, is slowly coming into town. Another, covered with the dust of travel, laden with bananas, hemp, and *copra* from a distant *barrio*, is being driven by a fellow in a *nipa* hat, straddling the heavy load. A mountain girl, bareheaded, carrying a parasol, comes loping in to the *mercado* on a skinny pony saddled with a red, upholstered *silla*, with a rattan back and foot-rest, cinched with twisted hemp.

At night the market-place is lighted up by tiny rush lights, burning cocoanut-oil or *petrolia*. Here, on a pleasant evening, to the lazy strumming of guitars, the village population promenades, young men in white holding each other's hands, and blowing out a cloud of cigarette smoke; *señoritas*, in their cheap red dresses, shuffling hopelessly along the road. One of the local characters is entertaining a street-corner audience with a droll song, while the town-crier, with his escort of municipal police, announces by the beating of a drum that a *bandilla* from the *presidente* is about to be pronounced.

Here you will find the Filipino in his natural and most playful mood, as easily delighted as a child. A crowd was always gathered round the *tuba* depot at the head of the *mercado*, where the agile climbers brought the beverage in wooden buckets from the tops of *copra*-trees. A comical old fellow, Pedro Pocpotoc (a name derived from chicken language), used to live here, and on moonlight nights, planting his fat feet on the window-sill, like a droll caricature of Nero, he would sing Visayan songs to the accompaniment of a cheap violin. A talkative old baker lived a short way down the street with his three daughters. They were always busy pounding rice in wooden mortars with long poles, thus making rice-flour, which they baked in clean banana-leaves and sweetened with brown sugar molded in the shells of cocoanuts.

Sometimes a Moro boat would drop into the bay, and the strange-looking savages in their tight-fitting, gaudy clothes would file through town with spices, bark, and cloth for sale. From Bohol came the curious thatched *bancas*, with their grass sails and bamboo outriggers, with cargoes of pottery, woven hats, *bohoka*, and rattan. On the *fiesta* days, Subanos from the mountains brought in strips of dried tobacco, ready to be rolled up into long cigars, *camotes*, coffee-berries, chocolate, and eggs, and squatted at the entrance to the cockpit in an improvised *mercado* with the people from the shore, who offered clams and *guinimos* for sale.

And once a month the town would be awakened by the siren whistle of the little hemp-boat from Cebu. This whistle was the signal for the small boys to extract the reluctant carabao from the cool, sticky wallow, and yoke him to the creaking bamboo cart. Then from the storehouses the fragrant *picos* of hemp would be piled on, and the longsuffering beast of burden, aided and abetted by a rope run through his nose, would haul the load down to the beach. While naked laborers were toiling with the cargo, carrying it upon their shoulders through the surf, the Spanish captain and the mate, with rakishly-tilted Tam o'Shanter caps, would light their cigarettes, stroll over to Ramon's warehouse where the hemp was being weighed, and, seated on sour-smelling sacks of *copra*, chat with old Ramon, partaking later of a dinner of *balenciona*, chicken and red-peppers, cheese and guava.

Much of the village life centers around the river. Here in the early morning come the girls and women wrapped in robes of red and yellow stripes, and with their hair unbound. In family parties the whole village takes a morning bath, the young men poising their athletic bodies on an overhanging bank and plunging down into the cool depths below, the children splashing in the shallow water, and the women breast-deep in the stream, washing their long hair.

Here also, during the morning hours, the women take their washing. Tying the *chemise* below the arms, they squat down near the shore and beat the wet mass with a wooden paddle on a rock. Meanwhile the children build extensive palaces of pebbles on the bank; the carabaos, up to their noses in the river, dream in the refreshing shade of overhanging trees. The air is vocal with the liquid notes of birds, and fragrant with the heavy scent of flowers. A leaf-green lizard creeps down on a horizontal trunk. The broad leaves of *abacá* rustle in the breeze; the graceful stalks of bamboo crackle like tin tubes. Around the bend the water ripples at the ford. At evening you will see the tired men from the mountains, bending under heavy loads of hemp, wade through the shallows to the cavern shelter of the banyan-tree. Through the dense mango-grove comes the faint sound of bells. The *puk-puk* bird hoots from the jungle, and the black crows settle in the lofty trees.

In a Visayan Village

The covered bridge that spans the river near the mouth is a great thoroughfare. Neither the arch nor pier is used in its construction; it is anchored to the shore by cables. It is not a very rigid bridge, and sways considerably when one is crossing it. Even the surefooted ponies step a little gingerly over the loose beams that form the floor. A curious procession is continually passing,—families moving their worldly goods on carabaos, the dogs and children following; *hombres* on ponies, grasping the stirrups with their toes; a padre with his gown caught up above his knees, riding away to some confession; mountain people traveling in single file, and girls with trays of merchandise upon their heads.

The Great White Tribe in Filipinia

Down where the *nipa* jungle thickens, fishing *bancas* are drawn up on the shore; and near by in a cocoanut-grove the old boatmaker lives. The hull of the outlandish boat that he is carving is a solid log. When finished, with its black paint, *nipa* gunwale, bamboo outriggers, and rat-lines made of parasitic vines, it will put out from port with a big gamecock as a mascot, rowed with clumsy paddles to the rhythm of a drum, its helpless grass sails flopping while the sailors whistle for the wind. These boats, although they can not tack, have one advantage—they can never sink. They carry bamboo poles for poling over coral bottoms. In a fair breeze they attain considerable speed; but there is danger in a heavy sea of swamping. When drawn up on shore they look like big mosquitoes, as the body in proportion to the rigging seems quite insignificant.

The little fishing village is composed of leaning shacks blown out of plumb by heavy winds. Along the beach on bamboo racks the nets are hanging out to dry. At night the little fleet puts out for Punta Gorda, where a ruined watch-tower—a protection against Moro pirates—stands half hidden among creeping vines. The nets are floated upon husks of cocoanut, and set in the wild light of burning rushes. While the men are working in the tossing sea, or venturing almost beyond sight of land, the women, lighting torches, wade out to the coral reef and seine for smaller fish among the rocks. Early the following morning, while the sea is gray, the fishermen will toss their catch upon the sand. The devil-fish are the most popular at the impromptu market, where the prices vary according to the run of luck.

The town was laid out by the Spaniards in the days when Padre Pedro was the autocrat and representative of Spanish law. The ruins of the former mission and the public gardens are now overgrown with grass. Sea-breezes sweep the rambling convent with its double walls, tiled courtyard, and its Spanish well. The new church, never to be finished, but with pompous front, illustrates the relaxing power of Rome. Goats, carabaos, and ponies graze on the neglected plaza shaded with widespreading camphor-trees. The two school buildings bearing the forgotten Spanish arms are on the road to ruin and decay; no signs of life in the disreputable *municipio*; the *presidente* probably is deep in his *siesta*, and the solitary guard of the *carcel* is busily engaged in conversation with the single prisoner.

The only remains of Spanish grandeur in the village are the two ramshackle coaches that are used for hearses at state funerals. Most of the larger houses are, however, in repair, although the canvas ceilings and the board partitions seem to be in need of paint. These houses occupy the center of the town. They are of frame construction, painted blue and white. The floors are made of rosewood and mahogany; the windows fitted with translucent shell. Storehouses occupy the first floor, while the living rooms are reached by a broad flight of stairs. A bridge connects the dining-room with the kitchen, where the greasy cook, often a Moro slave, works at a smoky fire of cocoanut-husks on an earth bottom, situated in an annex to the rear.

A walk through the main street leads past a row of native houses, built on poles and shaded by banana-trees. You are continually stepping over mats spread out and covered with pounded corn, while pigs and chickens are shooed off by the excitation of a piece of *nipa*, fastened to a string and operated from an upper window of the house. A small *tienda* opens from each house, with frequently no more than a few betel-nuts on sale. The front is decorated with the faded strips of cloth or paper lamps left over from the last *fiesta*, while the skeleton of a lamented monkey fixed above the door acts as a charm to keep away bad luck. A parrakeet swings in the window on a bamboo perch, and in another window hangs an orchid growing from the dried husk of a cocoanut. Under the house the loom is situated, where the women weave fine cloth from *piña* and banana fibers—and the wooden mortar used for pounding rice. After the harvest season it is one of the Visayan customs to inaugurate rice-pounding bees. Relays of young men, stripped for work, surround the mortar, and, to the accompaniment of guitars, deliver blows in quick succession and with gradually increasing speed, according to the measure of the music.

In the cool shade of the *ylang-ylang* tree a native barber is intent upon his customer. The customer sits on his haunches while the operation is performed. When it is finished, all the hair above the ears and neck will be shaved close, while that in front will be as long as ever. The beard will not need shaving, as the Filipino chin at best is hardly more aculeated than a strawberry. The hair, however, even of the smallest boys grows for some distance down the cheeks. The Filipino, when he does shave, takes it very seriously, and attacks the bristles individually rather than collectively.

You will not remain long in a Filipino town without the chance of witnessing a native funeral. A service of the first class costs about three hundred *pesos*; but for twenty *pesos* Padre Pedro will conduct a funeral of less magnificence. The padre, going to the house of mourning where the band, the singers, and the candle-bearers are assembled, engineers the pageant to the church. The dim interior will be illuminated by flickering candles burned in memory of the departed soul. Before the altar solemn mass is held, intensified by the deep tolling of a bell. Led by three acolytes in red and white, with silver crosses, the procession moves on to the cemetery on the outskirts of the town. The padre sheltered by a white umbrella, reads the Latin prayers aloud. A small boy swings the smoking censer, and the singers undertake a melancholy dirge. The withered body, with the hands crossed on the breast, clothed all in black, is borne aloft upon a bamboo litter, mounted with a black box painted with the skull and bones, and decked with candles. Women in black veils with candles follow, mumbling prayers, the words of which they do not understand.

The cemetery is surrounded by a coral wall, commanded by a gate that bears a Latin epigram. The graves, as indicated by the mounds of dirt, are never very deep, and while a few are guarded by a wooden cross, forlornly decorated by a withered bunch of flowers, most of the graves receive no care at all. There may be one or two vaults overgrown with grass and in a bad state of repair. Around the big cross in the center is a ghastly heap of human bones and grinning skulls—grinning because somebody else now occupies their former grisly beds, the rent on which has long ago expired.

To the Visayan mind, death is a matter of bad luck. It is advisable to hinder it with *anting-antings* and medallions; but when it comes, the

Filipino fatalist will take it philosophically. To the boys and girls a family death is the sensation of the year. It means to them nine days of celebration, when old women gather at the house, and, beating on the floor with hands and feet, put up a hopeless wail, while dogs without howl dismally and sympathetically. And at the end of the nine days, the soul then being out of purgatory, they will have a feast. A pig and a goat will be killed, not to speak of chickens—and the meat will be served up with calabash and rice; and visitors will come and look on while the people eat at the first table; and the second table and the third are finished, and the viands still hold out. But these are placed upon the table down below, where *hoi polloi* and the lame, blind, and halt sit down and eat. And back of all this superficiality lies the great superstitious dread by means of which the Church of Rome holds such authority.

I got to know the little village very well—to join the people in their foolish celebrations and their wedding feasts. I was among them when the town was swept by cholera; when, in their ignorance, they built a dozen little shrines—just *nipa* shelters for the Holy Virgin, decorated with red cloth and colored grass—and held processions carrying the wooden saints and burning candles.

Then the locusts came, and settled on the rice-fields—a great cloud of them, with whirring wings. They rattled on the *nipa* roofs like rain. The children took tin pans and drums and gave the enemy a noisy welcome. But the rains fell in the night, and the next morning all the ground was strewn with locusts trying heavily to fly. The ancient drum of the town-crier ushered in the day of work, and those who took this opportunity to pay their taxes gathered at the *municipio*— about a hundred ugly-looking men. They were equipped with working bolos, with their blades as sharp as scythes for cutting grass, and, looking at them, you were forcibly reminded of another day, another army with a similar accouterment. Even the *presidente* went barefooted as he gave directions for the work. Some were dispatched for *nipa* and bamboo, while others mowed the grass around the church. Another squad hauled heavy timbers, singing as they pulled in unison.

The Great White Tribe in Filipinia

On Sunday mornings a young carabao was killed. The meat hacked off with little reference to anatomy was hung up in the public stall among the swarms of flies. Old women came and handled every piece, and haggled a good deal about the price. Each finally selected one, and swinging it from a short piece of cane, carried it home in triumph. Morning mass was held at the big *simbahan*, where the doleful music of the band suggested lost souls wailing on the borders of Cocytus or the Stygian creek. Young *caballeros* dressed in white, the *concijales* with their silver-headed canes and baggy trousers, and the "*taos*" in diaphanous and flimsy shirts that they had not yet learned to tuck inside, stood by to watch the *señoritas* on their way to church. The girls walked rather stiffly in their tight shoes; but as soon as mass was over, shoes and stockings came off, and the villagers relaxed into the bliss of informality.

I learned, when I last went to *La Aurora*, that Felicidad was going to be married; that the banns had been announced last Sunday in the church. The groom to be, Benito,—or Bonito as we called him on account of his good looks,—had recently returned from college in Cebu, bringing a string of fighting cocks, a *fonografo*, and a piebald racing pony. "When he sent me the white ribbon," said Felicidad, "I was surprised, but mamma said that I was old enough to marry him— I was fourteen—and that the matter had been all arranged. And so I wore the ribbon in my hair, and also wrote my name *Felicidad* beneath his on the card that he had sent. And after that, when we went walking, the *dueña* was unnecessary."

She confessed naïvely to a serenade under her balcony, of which I seem to have retained a hazy memory. And so the usual pig and goat were roasted, and the neighbors' boys came in to help. The bride, with orange-blossoms in her hair, the daintiest kid slippers on her feet, and dressed in a white mist of *piña*, rode away in the new pony cart, the only one in town. The groom was dressed in baggy trousers, with a pink shirt and an azure tie. Most of the presents came from *Chino* Santiago's store; but the best one was a beautiful piano from Cebu.

After the service in the church, a feast was held upstairs in the bride's house. Ramon, the justice of the peace, the padre, *Maestro* Pepin, all the *concijales*, and the *presidente* were invited, and the groom owned up that he had spent his last cent on the refreshments that were passed around. It is the custom in the poorer families for the prospective groom to bond himself out for a certain length of time to the bride's father, or even to purchase her with articles of merchandise. A combination of commercial interests was the result, however, of the marriage of Bonito and Felicidad.

Chapter IX.
The "Brownies" of the Philippines.

How would you like it, not to have a Fourth of July celebration, or a Christmas stocking, or a turkey on Thanksgiving-day? The little children of the Philippines would be afraid of one of our firecrackers—they would think it was another kind of "boom-boom" that killed men. A life-sized turkey in the Philippines would be a curiosity, the chickens and the horses and the people are so small. The little boys and girls do not wear stockings, even around Christmas-time, and Santa Claus would look in vain for any chimneys over there. The candy, if the ants did not get at it first, would melt and run down to the toes and heels of Christmas stockings long before the little claimants were awake. Of course, they do not have plum-puddings, pumpkin-pies, and apples. All the season round, bananas take the place of apples, cherries, strawberries, and peaches; and boiled rice is the only kind of pumpkin-pie they have.

The fathers and mothers of the little Brownie boys and girls are very ignorant. Most of them can not even write their names, and if you asked them when the family birthdays came they would have to go and ask the padre. Once, when I was living at the convent, a girl-mother, who had walked in from a town ten miles away, came up to register the birth of a new baby in the padre's book. She stood before the priest embarrassed, digging her brown toes into a big crack in the floor. "At what time was the baby born?" was asked. "I do not know," she answered, "but it was about the time the chickens were awake."

It is a lucky baby that can get goat's milk to drink. Their mothers, living for the most part on dried fish and rice, are never strong enough to give them a good start in life. It is a common sight to see the tiny litter decorated with bright bits of paper and a half-dozen lighted candles, with its little, waxen image of a child, waiting without the church door till the padre comes to say the funeral services.

In that far-distant country but a small number of children ever have worn pretty clothes—only a tiny shirt; and they are perfectly contented, as the weather never gets uncomfortably cold. Their mothers or their older sisters carry them by placing them astride the hip, where they must cling tight with their little, fat, bare legs. They are soon old enough to run around and play; not on the grass among the trees, but in the dust out in the street. Their houses, built of *nipa* and bamboo, do not set back on a green lawn, but stand as near to the hot, dusty street as possible. To get inside the houses, which are built on posts, the babies have to scramble up a bamboo ladder, where they might fall off and break their necks. At this age they have learned to stuff themselves with rice until their little bodies look as though they were about to burst. A stick of sugar-cane will taste as good to them as our best peppermint or lemon candy. All the boys learn to ride as soon as they learn how to walk. Saddles and bridles are unnecessary, as they ride bareback, and guide the wiry Filipino ponies with a halter made of rope. The carabao is a great friend of Filipino boys and girls. He lets them pull themselves up by his tail, and ride him into town—as many as can make room on his back, allowing them to guide him by a rope run through his nose.

A Carabao

I do not think that many of the children can remember ever having learned to swim. The mothers, when they take their washing to the river, do not leave the little ones behind; and you can see their glistening brown bodies almost any morning at the riverside among the *nipa*, the young mothers beating clothes upon a rock, the carabaos up to their noses in the water, chewing their cuds and dreaming happy dreams. The boys can swim and dive like water-rats, and often remain in the river all day long.

The girls, when about five years old look very bright. Their hair is trimmed only in front (a good deal like a pony's), and their laughing eyes are very brown and mischievous. Most of them only wear a single ornament for a dress—a "Mother Hubbard" of cheap cotton print which they can buy for two *pesetas* at the *Chino* store. The boys all wear long trousers, and, at church or school, white linen coats, with military collars, which they call "*Americanas*," The girls do not wear hats. They save their "Dutchy" little bonnets, with the red and yellow paper flowers, for the *fiesta* days. They wear white veils on Sundays when they go to mass. The boys' hats often have long brims like those that we wear on the farm. They also have felt Tam o'Shanter caps, which they affect with quite a rakish tilt.

Playthings are scarce in Filipinia. The boys and girls would be delighted with a cheap toy cart or drum. The dolls are made of cotton cloth, with painted cheeks, and beads for eyes, dressed up in scraps of colored *piña* cloth in imitation of fine *señoritas*. Kite-time and the peg-top season come as in America. The Filipino kites are built like butterflies or birds, and sometimes carry a long beak which is of use in case of war. Kite-fighting is a favorite amusement in the islands, where the native boys are expert in the art of making and manipulating kites. Among the other games they play is one that an American would recognize as "tip-cat," and another which would be more difficult to recognize as football. This is played with a light ball or woven framework of rattan. The ball is batted from one player to another by the heel. The national pet is neither dog nor cat; it is a chicken and the grown-up people think almost as much of this unique pet as the children do.

Music comes natural to the Filipinos. Their instruments are violins, guitars, and flutes. The boys make flutes of young bamboo-stalks which are very accurate, and give out a peculiar mellow tone.

Fiesta-days and Sundays are the great events in Filipinia. On Sunday morning the young girls, in their white veils and clean dresses, go to mass, and, making the sign of the cross before the church, kneel down upon the bare tiles while the service is performed. The church to them is the magnificent abode of saints and angels. The wax images and altar paintings are the only things they have in art except the cheap prints of the saints and Virgin, which they hang conspicuously in their homes. *Pascua*, or Christmas week, is a great holiday, but it is very different from the Christmas that we know. The children going to the convent school are taught to sing the Spanish Christmas carols, and on Christmas eve they go outdoors and sing them on the streets in the bright starlight. Their voices, although untrained, are very delicate and sweet. The native music, which they often sing, like all the music of the southern isles, is very melancholy, often rising to a hopeless wail. On the last day of school the padre will distribute raisins, nuts, and figs, which are the only Christmas presents that the boys and girls receive. At the parochial schools they are taught to do their studying aloud, and always to commit the text to memory. If memory should fail them in a crisis, they would be extremely liable to have their ears pulled by the priest, or to be made to kneel upon the floor with outstretched arms, thus making the recitation somewhat of a tragedy; but there are also prizes for the meritorious. One book includes the whole curriculum—religion, table manners, grammar, "numbers," and geography—arranged in catechisms of convenient length. The boys are separated from the girls in school and church, and I have very seldom seen them play together in their homes. During the long vacation they must spend most of their time at work out in the rice-fields under the hot sun. So they would rather go to school than have vacation.

With the new schools and the American schoolteachers a great opportunity has come to the young people of the Philippines. New books with beautiful illustrations have been introduced, new songs, and a new way of studying. It would amuse you if you were to hear them read. "I do not see the pretty bird" they would pronounce, "Ee doa noat say day freety brud." The roll-call also sounds a good deal different from that in our own schools, where we have our Williams, Johns, and Henrys; but the Filipino names are very pretty (mostly names of Spanish saints), Juan, Mariano, Maximo, Benito, and Torribio for boys; Carnation, Bernarda, and Adela for the girls. The boys especially are very bright, and they are learning rapidly, not only grammar and arithmetic, but how to play baseball and tag and other games that make the child-life of America so pleasant.

Chapter X.
Christmas in Filipinia.

While you are in a land of starlight, frost, and sleighbells, here the cool wind brushes through the palms and the blue sea sparkles in the sun. "In every Christian kind of place" it is the time of Christmas bells and Christmas masses. Even at the Aloran convent—about the last outpost of civilization (only a little way beyond live the wild mountain folk—sun-worshipers and the Mohammedans) the padre has prepared a treat of nuts and raisins for the boys and girls— somewhat of a Christmas cheer even so far across the sea. They have been practicing their Christmas songs, Ave Maria and the "Oratorio," which they will sing around the streets on Christmas eve. The schoolboys have received their presents—dictionaries, sugared crackers, and perfumed soap—and now that their vacation has begun, their little brown heads can be seen bobbing up and down in the blue sea. Their Christmas-tree will be the royal palm; and *nipa* boughs their mistletoe.

Last Christmas in the provinces I spent in Iloilo at a hostel kept by a barefooted Spanish landlady, slovenly in a loose morning-gown and with disheveled hair, who stored the eggs in her own bedroom and presided over the untidy staff of house-boys. As she usually slept late, we breakfasted without eggs, being limited to chocolate and cakes. The only option was a glass of lukewarm coffee thinned to rather sickening proportions with condensed milk. Dinner, however, was a more elaborate affair, consisting of a dozen courses, which began with soup and ended with bananas or the customary cheese and guava. The several meat and chicken courses, the "*balenciona*" — boiled rice mixed with chicken giblets and red peppers—and the bread, baked hard and eaten without butter, was washed down with a generous glass of *tinto* wine. A pile of rather moist plates stood in front of you, and as you finished one course an untidy thumb removed the topmost plate, thus gradually diminishing the pile.

The dining-room was very interesting. A pretentious mirror in a tarnished gilt frame was the *piece de resistance*. The faded chromos of the royal family, the Saints, and the Enfanta were relieved by the brilliant lithographs presenting brewers' advertisements. A majestic chandelier, considerably fly-specked, but elaborately ornamented with glass prisms, dropped from the frescoed ceiling, and a cabinet containing miscellaneous seashells, family photographs, and starfish occupied one corner of the room.

There was a Christmas eve reception at the home of the "Dramatic Club," where the refreshments of cigars and anisette and bock beer were distributed with liberal hand. The Filipino always does things lavishly. The evening was devoted to band concerts—the municipal band in the pavilion rendering the Mexican waltzes, "Over the Waves," "The Dove," and other favorites, while the "upper ten" paraded in the moonlight under the mimosa-trees—serenades under the Spanish balconies, and carol-singing to the strumming of guitars. The houses were illumined with square tissue paper lanterns of soft colors. The public market was a fairyland of light. The girls at the tobacco booths offered a special cigarette tied with blue ribbon as a souvenir of the December holidays. A mass at midnight was conducted in the venerable church. As the big bronze bells up in the belfry tolled the hour the auditorium was filled with worshipers— women in flapping slippers and black veils; girls smelling of cheap perfumery and cocoanut-oil, in their stiff gauze dresses with the butterfly sleeves; barefooted boys and young men redolent of cigarettes and musk. A burst of music from the organ in the loft commenced the services, which were concluded with the passing of the Host and a selection by the band. The priest on this occasion wore his gold-embroidered chasuble; the acolytes, red surplices and lace.

The streets next morning—Christmas-day—were thronged with merry-makers. Strangers from the mountain tribes, wild, hungry-looking creatures, had strayed into town, not only for the excitement of the cockpit, but to do their trading and receive their share of alms, which are distributed by all good Catholics at this season of the year.

Here on the corner was a great wag in an ass's head, accomplishing a clumsy dance for the amusement of the crowd. Around the cockpit chaos was the order of the day. The eager fighting-cocks, in expectation of the combat, straining at their tethers, published to the world their lusty challenges. The "talent," with delicious thrills, were hefting favorite champions, and hastening' to register their wagers with the bank.

The cock-fights lasted the entire week; at the end of that time the erratic "wheel of fortune" had involved in ruin many an enthusiast who had unfortunately played too heavily the losing bird.

A strolling troop of actors came to visit us that night. They carried their own scenery and wardrobe with them, and the children who were to present the comedy were dressed already for the first act. As they filed in, followed by a mob of ragamuffins who had seen the show a dozen times or more without apparent diminution of enjoyment, the stage manager arranged the scenery and green-room, which consisted of a folding screen. The orchestra, with bamboo flutes, guitars, and mandolins, took places on a bench, where they began the overture, beating the measure with bare feet and with as much delight as though they were about to witness the performance for the first time. The proprietor informed us that the entertainment was to be a comedy of old Toledo. It was somewhat of a Cyrano de Bergerac affair; one of the principals, concealed behind the "leading man," using his own arms for gestures, sang his representative love for the señorita in the Spanish dancer's costume. The castanet dance was repeatedly encored, especially by those familiar with the program, who desired that we appreciate it to its full extent. The actors in this dance were dressed as Spanish buccaneers are popularly supposed to dress, in purple breeches buttoned at the knee, red sashes, and gold lace....

Last night at our own church three paper lanterns, shaped like stars and representing the "three wise men," at the climax of the mass were worked on wires so that they floated overhead along the auditorium, and finally came to rest above the altar, which had been transformed into a manger, the more realistic on account of the pigs, ducks, and chickens manufactured out of paper that had been disposed around.

To-day three men in red are traveling from house to house with candles followed by an attendant with a bell, ringing away the evil spirits for a year. The councilmen in snowy blouses and blue pantaloons, with their official canes, are making their official calls, and Padre Pedro in his pony cart has been around to visit his parishioners. The band, equipped with brand new uniforms and instruments, is playing underneath the convent balcony. Their duties during the festivities are strenuous; for they must serenade the residence of every magnate in the town, receiving contributions of *pesetas*, cigarettes, and gin.

This afternoon we made our round of calls, for every family keeps open house. A number of matinée balls were in session, where the natives danced "clack-clack" around the floor to the monotonous drone of home-made instruments. Our friends all wished us a *"Ma-ayon Pascua"* or *"Feliz Pascua,"* for which "Merry Christmas" they expected some remembrance of the day. Our efforts were rewarded by innumerable gifts of cigarettes and many offers of *tanduay* and gin. At one place we experimented with a piece of *"bud-bud,"* which is (as its name implies) a sweet-meat made of rice paste mixed with sugar. The hams with sugar frosting, and the cakes flavored with native limes, and cut in the shape of the "Ensanguined Heart," were more acceptable. At one house we received a cake made in the image of a lamb, with sugar ringlets representing fleece. At our departure, "many thanks, sir, for the visit," and a final attempt to get rid of another cigarette. It is in bad taste to refuse. A Filipino host would feel offended at your not accepting what he offered. He would feel as though discrimination were implied.

At night after the cock-fight one droll fellow brought around a miniature marionette theater, of which he was the proud proprietor. While his assistant blew a bamboo flute behind the scenes, the puppets danced fandangoes and played football in a very lifelike manner. Seated on an empty cracker-box in front, surrounded by the ragged picaninnies, sat Dolores, with her sparkling eyes, lips parted, and her black hair hanging loose,—oblivious to everything except the marionettes.

The star attraction was preceded by applause. The number was announced by those familiar with the exhibition as a "Moro combat," and as the assistant struck a harrowing obligato on an old oil-can, the Moros appeared with fighting *campalons* and barbarous-looking shields. The crowd expressed its approbation in wild howls. The first two rounds were rather tame. "Afraid! Afraid!" exclaimed the crowd, but presently the combatants began to warm up to their work and to make frantic lunges at each other at the vital spot. This was the time of breathless and instinctive pressing forward from the back rows. Somebody cried out, "*Cebu!*" or "Down in front!" and then again, "*Patai!*" which means "dead." One of the warriors at this cue flopped supine on the stage, and the suppressed excitement broke. The victor, not content with mere manslaughter, plied his sword so energetically as quickly to reduce his victim to a state of hash. At this point his Satanic majesty, the curtain manager, saw fit to intervene, and with a long spear he successfully probed the limp remains, completing the assassination. I had not known until then what a young barbarian Dolores was.

The last attraction of our Christmas week was a genuine Mystery play, the Virgin Mary being represented by a girl in soiled white stockings and a confirmation dress. The Christ Child was a Spanish doll in a glass case. There were the three wise men—one in a long beard and a pink mask, and the others in gold braid and knickerbockers—more like dandies than philosophers. "Joseph" was splendid, with a shepherd's crook and a sombrero. Adoration before the manger was the theme that was developed in a series of ballets danced by the children to a tambourine and castanet accompaniment. At the conclusion of the play, the little actors in their starry costumes, Joseph and the Virgin (carrying the Babe), the three philosophers, and the musicians and the army of admiring followers, filed out into the moonlight, and as the sweet music of the "Shepherds' Song" diminished gradually, they disappeared within a shadowy grove of palms.

A Christmas Feast.

When Señor Pedro gave his Christmas feast, he went about it in the orthodox way. That is, he began at midnight Christmas eve. The Christmas pig we were to have had, however, disappointed us—and thereby hangs a tale.

Came Señor Pedro early in the morning of the twenty-fourth, and "In the mountains," Señor Pedro said, "runs a fat pig." *Usa ca babui uga dacu!* A regular feast of a pig running at large near the macao woods on the slope beyond Mercario's hemp-fields!

Nothing would do but that I buckle on my Colt's—a weapon that I had done much destruction with among the lesser anthropoids in the vicinity. Then we set out radiantly for the hills, with Señor Pedro leading and a municipal policeman with us to take home the pig. We soon arrived at the pig's stamping grounds. We had not long to wait. There was a snapping of the underbrush, and "Mr. Babui" appeared upon the scene. His great plank side and sagging belly was as fair a mark as any sportsman could have wished. His greedy little eyes were fixed upon the ground where he was rooting for his Christmas dinner.

Bang! The bullet from the army Colt's sped true. Our pig, flat on his back, was squealing desperately, and his feet were pawing the air as last as though he had been run by clockwork and had been suddenly released from contact with the ground. Then the municipal policeman went to pick him up. But lo, a miracle! Our Christmas pig, inspired by supersusine terror on the approach of the dire representative of law, regained his legs, and before we could recover from our astonishment, had scudded away with an expiring squeak like that emitted from a musical balloon on its collapse. We never found the pig. He was just mean enough to die in privacy.

But there was to be some compensation. What, though our Christmas dinner had escaped? I managed to bring down a monkey that for some time had been chattering and scolding at us from a tree, and with this substitute—a delicacy rare to native palates—marched triumphantly back to the town.

Exactly at midnight the *señores* took their seats around the board. The orchestra was stationed in an elevated alcove in the next room. On the benches sat the women, from the dainty Juliana in her pink cotton hosiery and white kid slippers to the old witch Paola, the town scold. We knives or forks. Heaping platefuls of rice were served with the stewed meat—cut in small pieces that "just fit the hand," and cooked with vegetables. At my request the monkey had been roasted whole. "All la same bata" (baby) cried my host, and sure, I never felt more like a cannibal in all my life. I shuddered later when, the ladies at the table, Juliana gnawed the thigh-bone of the little beast with relish.

Señor Pedro kept the orchestra supplied with gin, with the result that what they lacked in accuracy they made up for in enthusiasm. In the dim room, lighted only by the smoky "kinkes," we could see the hungry eyes of those awaiting the third table—the retainers and the poor relations. On the boards below was spread a banquet of rice and *tuba* for the multitude.

The party broke up with a dance, and as the pointers of the Southern Cross faded from the pale sky, the happy merrymakers filed off to their beds. They had so little in this far-off corner of the world, and yet they were content. Had not the stars looked down upon them through the tropic night? Had not the blue sea broken in phosphorescent ridges at their feet? And didn't they have the Holy Virgin on the walls to smile a blessing on their little scene of revelry? O, it was Christmas over all the world! And on this day at least the white man and the "little brown brother" could shake hands over mutual interests.

Chapter XI.
In a Visayan Home.

The shutters of the house across the street were closed. Under the balcony, near where the road was strewn with scarlet blossoms from the fire-tree, carpenters were hammering and sawing busily. Shaped by the antiquated bandsaw and the bolos, a rude coffin gradually assumed its grim proportions. A group of schoolboys, drawn by curiosity, looked on indifferently while keeping up a desultory game of tag. Upstairs, the women, dressed in the black veils of mourning, shuffling noiselessly around, were burning candles at the "Queen of Heaven's" shrine. They murmured prayers mechanically—not without a certain reverence and awe—to usher the departing soul into the land beyond. A smoky wall-lamp, glimmering near the door, illuminated the black crucifix above the bed. In the dim candle-light vague shadows danced on the white walls.

The priest had heard the last confession of José Pilar. Not that José had been one of the padre's friends. In fact, he was suspected during the past year of having been a secret agent of Aglipay, the self-consecrated Bishop of Manila, and the target of the accusation and invective that the Church of Rome is so proficient in. The recent rulings of the order had abolished the confession fee; but the long road was uncertain and the dangers great. The padre rubbed his hands as he went out. He had received a "voluntary" contribution for his services, with the assurance that a series of masses would be ordered by the widow of José Pilar. Through the stiff palms, the cold sea, gray as steel, washed the far-distant shores of lonely islands, and the red glow of the setting sun had died away.

The padre thought about the plump goats and the chickens in the new stockade. The simple people brought their chickens to the convent, denying themselves all but the fish and rice. The mothers weaned their puny brats on rice; they stuffed them with it till their swollen paunches made a grotesque contrast with their skinny legs. Childbirth is one of the minor incidents of Filipinia. Where is the house that doesn't swarm with babies, like the celebrated residence of the old woman in the shoe? When one of these sparrows falls, the little song that dies is never missed.

How many times had Father Cipriano climbed the rickety ladder to the *nipa* dwellings, entering the closed room where the patient lay upon the floor! A gaping crowd of yokels stood around, while the old woman faithfully kneaded the abdomen. The native medicaster, having placed the green leaves on the patient's temples, would be brewing a concoction of emollient simples. The open shirt disclosed upon the patient's breast the amulet which had been blessed by Padre Cipriano, and was stamped with a small figure of a saint. The holy father smiled as he reflected how they spent their last cent for the funeral ceremonies, while the doctor's fee would be about a dozen eggs. And even now that death had come to one not quite so ignorant and simple as the rest, the funeral celebrations would be but the more elaborate. Not every one who could afford a coffin in Malingasag! And as the padre crossed the *plaza* he lighted a cigarette.

It was with feelings of annoyance that he saw before the side door of the church a tiny litter cheaply decorated with bright paper and red cloth. The yellow candles threw a fitful light over the little image on the bier. It was the image of a child, a thing of wax, clothed in a white dress, with a tinsel crown upon its head. One of the sacristans was drumming a tattoo upon the bells. The padre motioned him to discontinue. He would have his gin-and-water first, and then devotions, lasting twenty minutes. After devotions he could easily dispose of the small child. So the two humble women waited in patience at the door, and the cheap candles sputtered and went out before the good priest could find time to hurry through the unimportant funeral services that meant to him only a dollar or two at best in the depreciated silver currency. Already night was overshadowing the palm-groves as the pathetic little group filed out and trudged across the rice-pads toward the cemetery.

The Filipinos regard the American doctors with suspicion. When a snakebite can be cured by a burnt piece of carabao horn, or when the leaves or bits of paper stuck upon the temple will relieve the fever or the dysentery, what is the use of drugs and medicines and things that people do not understand? Once, out of the kindness of his heart, an army doctor that I knew, prescribed a valuable ointment for a child afflicted by a running sore. The child was in a terrible condition, as the sore had eaten away the flesh and bone, leaving a large hole under the lower lip through which the roots of the teeth were all exposed. The parents had not washed the child for weeks. They actually believed that bathing was injurious when one was sick. The doctor, giving them directions how to use the medicine, asked them, as an experiment, what fee he might expect. He knew well that if the priest had asked this question, they would eagerly have offered everything they had. So he was not surprised when they replied that they were very poor, and that they did not think the service was worth anything. The doctor turned them away good naturedly, but they returned the next day with the medicine, reporting that undoubtedly it was no good, because, forsooth, the child had cried when they applied it! As a peace-offering they brought a dozen miserable bananas.

Slinging a tablet around his neck, a "valuable remedy against the pest," the Filipino thinks that he is reasonably secure against disease, and that if he becomes afflicted, it is the result of some transgression against heaven. I happened to receive a startling proof, however, of its efficacy when the padre's house-boy, rather a bright young fellow, made me a present of his "remedy" and died the next day of cholera. Still I have seen the *"anting-anting,"* which is supposed to render the wearer bullet-proof, pierced with the balls of the Krag-Jorgensen and stained with blood. Although the Visayans show considerable sympathy toward one when he is sick, the native dentist cutting out the tooth with a dull knife, we would consider almost too barbarous to practice in America. The Igorrotes have a way of driving out the fever with a slow fire; but between this Spartan method and Visayan ignorance the choice is difficult. No wonder that the people drop off with surprising suddenness. Your laundryman or baker fails to come around some morning, and you ask one of your neighbors where he is. The neighbor, shifting his wad of *buya* to the other cheek, will gradually wake up and answer something ending in *"ambut." "Ambut"* is a convenient word for the Visayan, as it means "don't know," and even if he is informed, the Filipino often is too lazy or indifferent to explain. You finally discover some one more accommodating who replies: "Why, haven't you heard? He died the other day."

Sulkiness, one of the characteristics of the girls and boys, develops into surliness in men and billingsgate in women. And I have no doubt that little Diega, the sulkiest and prettiest of the Visayan beauties, in a few years will be gambling at the cock-fights, smoking cigars, and losing her money every Sunday afternoon at Mariana's *monte* game. Vulgarity with them goes down as wit, and the Visayan women make a fine art of profanity. It is always the woman in a family quarrel who is most in evidence. And even the delicate Adela when the infant Richard fell downstairs the other day, cried, "Mother of God!" which she considered to be more appropriate than *"Jesus, Marie, Josep!"*

On entering one of the common houses, you would be astonished at the pitiable lack of furnishings. The floor is made of slats of split bamboo, tied down with strips of cane. The walls are simply the dried *nipa* branches, fastened down with bamboo laths. The only pictures on the walls are the cheap prints of saints, the "Lady of the Rosary," or illustrations clipped together with the reading matter from some stray American magazine. The picture of a certain popular shoe manufacturer is sometimes given the place of honor near the crucifix. If any attempt at decoration has been made, the lack of taste of the Visayans is at once apparent. For the ancient fly-specked chromo of the "Prospect of Madrid" is as artistic in their eyes as though the advertisement of a certain cracker factory did not adorn the margin. The undressed pillars that support the house, run through the floor. The *nipa* shutters that protect the windows are propped open, making heavy awnings, and permitting a free circulation of the breeze. There are no ceilings in these houses, and the entire framework of the roof is visible. A cheap red curtain, trimmed with lace, is draped before the entrance to the sleeping-room. While in the better frame-constructed residences an old Spanish tester bed with a cane bottom may be seen in this apartment, here only the straw mats and the cotton bolsters are to be found. A basket hanging from a bamboo spring serves as a cradle for the baby, but it is a pretty lucky baby that indulges in this luxury, as most of the children, spreading the mats upon the floor at night, pillow their heads upon the bolsters, ten in a row, and go to sleep. A marble-topped table and a few chairs, formally arranged as though in preparation for a conclave, are the features of the larger homes; but generally the furniture consists of a long bench, a wooden table, and a camphorwood box, which contains the family treasures, and the key to which the woman of the house wears in her belt—a symbol of authority.

On climbing the outside stairway to the living-rooms you find your passage blocked by a small fence. In trying to step over this you nearly crush a naked baby, and a yellow dog snaps venomously at your heels. You enter the main room, where the pony-saddle and the hemp-scales may be stored. The Filipinos are great visitors, and you will find a ring of old men squatting upon the benches like so many hens, chewing the betel-nut and nursing their enormous feet. Some fellow in the corner, with a chin like a sea-urchin, strums a tune monotonously on an old guitar. Your host arises, offers you a glass of gin and a cigar or cigarette, and asks you to "*lincoot dinhi.*" So, at his invitation, you sit down, and are expected to begin the conversation. Such conversation is enlightening and runs somewhat like this:

"Yes, thank you, I am very well; Yes, we are all well. Everything is well.... The beer of the Americans is very good.... Whisky is very strong.... The Filipino whisky is not good for anything.... It is very dull here. It is not our custom to have pretty girls.... What is your salary? All the Americans are very rich. We are all very poor.... The horses in America are very large. Why?... If the people want me, I will be elected mayor. But let them decide.... After a while will you not let me have some medicine? The wife has beri-beri very bad."

The family arises with the chickens. For the Filipino boy no chores are waiting to be done. The ponies and the dogs are never fed. Nobody seems to care much for the animals. With the exception of the fighting-cock, chickens, dogs, pigs, and carabaos are left to forage for themselves. The pigs and dogs are public scavengers, and the poor curs that howl the night long, till you wish that they were only allowed to bay the moon in daytime, stalk the barren shores or rice-pads in the hope of preying upon carrion. A Filipino dog, though pinched and starved, has not the courage even to catch a young kid by the ear, and much less to say "boo" to a goose. It is surprising how the ponies, feeding upon the coarse grass, ever become as wiry as they do. Evidently, to the Filipino, animals do not have feelings; for they often ride their ponies furiously, though the creature's back may be a running sore. In using wooden saddles they forget to place a pad beneath them, and the saddle thus becomes an instrument of torture.

After the morning bath in the cool river, a cup of chocolate or a little bowl of rice will serve for breakfast. Then the women attend morning mass and kneel for half an hour on the hard tiles. It is still early in the day, and the fantastic mountains, with their wonderful lights and shadows, are just throwing off the veil of mist. Now, in the clear light, the huge, swelling bosom of the hills, the densely-timbered slopes beyond, stand out distinctly, like a picture in a stereoscope. The heavy forests, crowded with gigantic trees, seem like a mound of bushes thickly bunched. Off to the left rises a barren ridge, that might have been the spine of some old reptile of the mezozoic age; and in the center a Plutonic ampitheater—the council-chamber of the gods—is swept by shadows from the passing clouds, or glorified for a brief moment by a flood of light.

The boys are then sent out to catch one of the ponies for their father, who is going to inspect his hemp plantation on the foot-hills. His progress will at first be rather slow; for he is a great chatterbox, and if he finds some crony along the road, he will dismount and drink a glass of *tuba* with him, or dicker with him over an exchange of fighting cocks. The birds are then brought out, and the two men squat down, with the birds in hand, and set them pecking at each other to display their fine points. But the string of *hombres*, with their bolos slung about their waists, making for the mountains, reminds the planter that he must be getting on. His fields are let out to these fellows, who will pay him a proportion of the hemp which they can strip. Although the process of preparing hemp is primitive and slow, the green stalk being stripped by an iron comb, the laboring man can prepare enough in one day to supply his family with "*sow sow*" for an entire week. If he would work with any regularity, especially in the wild hemp-fields, he would soon be "independent," and could buy the hemp from others, which could be sold at a profit to the occasional hemp-boats that come into port. The only capital required is one or two bull-carts and carabaos, a storehouse, and sufficient rice or money to secure his first invoice of hemp. The men who carry it in from the mountains, either on their own backs or on carabaos, sell it for cash or its equivalent in rice at the first store.

On Saturdays, the boys go to the mountains to buy eggs. Their first stop is the *hacienda* on the outskirts of the town—a large, cool *nipa* house, with broad verandas, situated in a grove of palms. Around the veranda are the nests of woven baskets where the chickens are encouraged to lay eggs. Sucking a juicy mango, they proceed upon their journey through a field of sugar-cane. They stop perhaps at the rude mill where the brown sugar is prepared and molded in the shells of cocoanuts. They quench their thirst here with a stick of sugar-cane, and, peeling the sweet stalk with their teeth, they disappear beyond the hill. Now they have reached a wonderful country, where the monkeys and the parrots chatter in the trees. They can set traps for little parrots with a net of fine thread fastened to the branches. Only a little further on is a small mountain *barrio*, where naked, lazy men lie in the sun all day, and the women weave bright-colored blankets on their looms. Returning with their handkerchiefs tied full of eggs, the boys reach home about sundown. The thought of being late to supper never worries them; the Filipino is notoriously unpunctual at meals. The boys will cook their own rice, and spread out the sleeping-mat wherever the sunset finds them. One shelter is as good as another, and they just as often sleep away from home as in their own beds. Their parents never worry about the children, for they know that, like Bo-peep's sheep, they will come back some time, and it doesn't make much difference when.

Early in April the rice-fields are flooded by the irrigation ditches that the river or the mountain streams have filled with water. A plow made of the notch of a tree is used to break the soil. A carabao is used for this work, as it is impossible to mire him even in the deepest mud. The boys and girls, together with the men and women, wearing enormous sun-hats—in the crown of which there is a place for cigarettes and matches—and with bared legs, work in the steaming fields throughout the planting season. As the rice grows taller, the crows are frightened away by strings of flags manipulated from a station in the center of the paddy. Scarecrows are built whenever there are any clothes to spare; but as the Filipino even utilizes rags, the scarecrow often has to go in shocking *négligée*. After the harvest season, when the entire village reaps the rice with bolos, the dry field is given over to the ponies, and the carabaos, and the white storks, who never desert their burly friend, the carabao, but often are seen perching on his back. The work of husking and pounding the crop then occupies the village.

If you should be invited in to dinner by a Filipino family, you would expect to eat boiled rice and chicken. They would place a cuspidor on one side of your chair to catch the chicken bones, which you would spit out from your mouth. The food would be cooked in dishes placed on stones over an open fire. The cook and the *muchachos* never wash their hands. They wash the dishes only by pouring some cold water on them and letting them dry gradually. The cook will rinse the glasses with his hand. How would you like to eat a chicken boiled with its pin-feathers on, or find a colony of red ants in your soup? The poorer families seldom go through the formality of serving meals. As soon as the rice and *guinimos* are cooked, the children and their parents squat around the bowl and help themselves, holding a lump of salt in one hand, and using the other for a fork or spoon. The women do what little marketing needs to be done, and though the Filipino acts in most things lavishly, the women can drive close bargains, and will scold like ale-wives if they find the measure short even by so much as a single *guinimo*.

The *guinimo* is probably the smallest creature with a vertebra known to the world of science—a small fish—and it strikes one as amusing when the people count them out so jealously. But all their marketing is done on retail lines. Potatoes, eggs, and fruit sell for so much apiece. A single fish will be chopped up so as to go around among the customers, while the measures used in selling rice and salt are so small that you can not take them seriously. The transaction reminds you of your childhood days when you were playing "keep store" with a nickel's worth of candy on the ironing-board.

At Easter-time, or during the celebration of the "Santa Cruz," an enterprising family will get up a singing bee. Perhaps a wheezy organ will be brought to light, and the musician then officiates behind the instrument. His bare feet work the pedals vigorously, and his body sways in rhythm with the strains. As the performance is continuous, arriving or departing guests do not disturb the ceremony. There seems to be a special song for this occasion, the words of which must be repeated over and over as the music falls and rises in a dismal wail. Refreshments of Holland gin and *tuba* keep the party going until long after midnight.

As you walk down the long dusty street at evening, you will be half suffocated by the smoke and the rank odor of the burning cocoanut-husks over which the supper is being cooked. Then you remember how the broiling beefsteak used to smell "back home," and even dream about grandmother's kitchen on a baking day. And as you pass by the poor *nipa* shacks, you hear the murmur of the evening prayer pronounced by those within. It is a prayer from those who have but little and desire no more.

Chapter XII.
Leaves from a Note-book.

I.

Skim Organizes the Constabulary.

The soldiers had gone, bag and baggage, dog, parrot, and monkey, blanket-roll and cook. I stood by the deserted convent under the lime-tree, watching the little transport disappear beyond the promontory. The house that formerly had been headquarters seemed abandoned. There was the list of calls still pasted on the door. Reveille, guard-mount, mess-call, taps,—the village would seem strange without these bugle-notes. The sturdy sentry who had paced his beat was gone. When would I ever see again my old friend the ex-circus clown, and hear him tinkle the "potato-bug" and sing "Ma Filipino Babe?" Walking along the lonely shore, now lashed by breakers, I looked out on the blue wilderness beyond. It was with feelings such as Robinson Crusoe must have had that I went back then to the empty house.

Ramon, convinced that something would break loose, now that the troops were gone, had left for Cagayan. His wife, Maria, slept at night with a big bolo underneath her pillow. There was a "bad" town only a few miles away—a village settled by Tagalog convicts, who had been conspicuous in the revolt a few years previous. The people feared these neighbors, the assassins, and they double-barred their doors at night. I was awakened as the clock struck twelve by unfamiliar noises,—nothing but the lizard croaking in the bonga-tree. Again, at one, I started up. It was the rats, and from the rattling sound above I judged that the house-snake was pursuing them. At early morning came the chorus of the chanticleers. Through the transparent Japanese blinds I could see the huge green mountains shouldering the overhanging clouds. Ah! the mysterious, silent mountains, with their wonderful, deep shadows! The work of man seemed insignificant beside them, and Balingasag the lonesomest place in all the world.

The Great White Tribe in Filipinia

One morning the sharp whistle of the launch aroused the town. Proceeding to the shore, I saw a boat put out from the *Victoria*, sculled by a native deck-hand. As the sun had not yet risen, all the sea was gray, and sea and sky blended into one vast planetary sphere. Two natives carrying the ample form of the constabulary captain staggered through the surf. Behind them came the captain's life-long partner and lieutenant, a slight man, with cold, steely eyes, dressed in gray crash uniform, with riding leggings. They had been through one campaign together as rough riders; for the captain had once been "sheriff of Gallup County," in the great Southwest.

The house no longer seemed deserted with this company, and as they had brought supplies for two months—which included bread!—we made an early attack upon these commissaries. Since the troops had left I had been existing on canned salmon and sardines. Now there were cheese, guava, artichokes, mushrooms, ham, bacon, blackberry-jam, and fruits. The captain, natural detective that he was, caught one of the *muchachos* stealing a bottle of cherries, which he had thrown out the window during the unpacking, with the purpose of securing it next day. On being accused, he made a vigorous protest of his innocence, but after a few minutes he returned triumphantly with the intelligence that he had "found" that which was lost.

A heavy rain and the tail-end of a monsoon kept my two guests prisoners for a week. The *presidente* of the town had issued a *bandilla* that all able-bodied men were wanted to enlist in the constabulary. Accordingly came awkward natives to the house, where the interpreter examined them; for all the Spanish that the genial captain knew—and he had lived already two years in the Philippines—was "bueno," "malo," "saca este," and "sabe that?" The candidates were measured, and, if not found wanting, were turned over to the native tailor to be fitted with new uniforms. Some of the applicants confessed that they had once been Insurrectos; but so much the better,—they knew how to fight. They said that they were not afraid of Moros—though I think that they would rather have encountered tigers—and when finally dressed, a few days later, they appeared upon the streets self-conscious, objects of adoration in the eyes of all the local belles.

The time came when the mists dissolved upon the mountains, and the little clouds scudded along overhead as though to get in from the rain. The sun had struggled out for a few minutes, and the wind abated. But the sea had not forgotten recent injuries, and all night we could hear the booming of the surf. The launch, drowned in a nebula of spray, dashed by, and sought an anchorage in safer waters. So it was decided that we go to Cagayan in a big *banca*. But it was a most unwieldly craft to launch. We got the arms and ammunition safe aboard, and then, assisted by the sturdy corporals and miscellaneous natives, we pushed out. A rushing comber swept the boat and nearly swamped it. But we bore up till about a hundred yards from shore, when a gigantic breaker bearing down upon the *banca*—which had been deflected so as to present a broadside—filled her completely, and she went down in the swirling spume. Up to our necks in surf, we labored for an hour, together with the population of the fishing village, finally to save the wretched boat and most of the constabulary ordnance.

But, alas for the lieutenant! He had lost one of his riding-leggings, and for half a day he paced the shore in search of it. He offered rewards to any native who should rescue it. Lacking a saving sense of humor, he bemoaned his fate, and when he did give up the search, he discontinued it reluctantly. And two years afterwards, when I next met him, he inquired if I had seen his legging washed up on the beach. "Some native must be sporting around in it," he said. "It set me back five dollars, Mex."

It was a sleepy day at Cagayan. The tropical river flowed in silence through the jungle like a serpent. In *Capitan* A-Bey's house opposite, a *señorita* droned the *Stepanie Gavotte* on the piano. *Capitan* A-Bey's pigs rooted industriously in the compound. The teacher who had hiked in from El Salvador, unconscious that his canvas leggings were transposed, was engaged in a deep game of solitaire.

Upon the settee in the new constabulary residence, his long legs doubled up ridiculously, still in khaki breeches and blue flannel army shirt, lay "Skim," with a week's growth of beard upon his face, sleeping after a night-ride over country roads. After an hour or two of rest he would again be in the saddle for two days.

Late in the afternoon we started on constabulary ponies for Balingasag—a ride of thirty miles through quagmires, over swollen streams and mountain trails. Our ponies were the unaccepted present from a quack who thus had tried to buy his way out of the calaboose, where he was "doing time" for trying to pass himself off as a prophet.

The first few miles of the journey led through the cloistered archways of bamboo. We crossed the Kauffman River, swimming the horses down stream. Then the muddy roads began. The constant rains had long ago reduced them to a state of paste, and although some attempt had been made to stiffen them with a filling of dried cocoanut-husks, the sucking sound made by the ponies' hoofs was but a prelude to our final floundering in the mud. There was a narrow ridge on one side near a thorny hedge, and, balancing ourselves on this, we made slow progress, meanwhile tearing our clothes to shreds. Skim had considerable difficulty with his long legs, for he could have touched the ground on either side, but he could use them to advantage, when it came to wading through the slosh ourselves, and dragging the tired ponies after us. At night we "came to anchor" in a village, where we purchased a canned dinner in a Spanish store. The natives gathered around us as we sat, all splashed with mud, on wicker chairs in front of the provincial *almacen*. Skim talked with the Spaniard, alternating every word with "*estie*," while the Don kept swallowing his eyes and gesturing appropriately. Skim was convinced that his Castilian was fine art.

We slept in a deserted schoolhouse, lizards and mosquitoes being our bed-fellows. Skim, the rough cowboy that he was, pillowed his head upon the horse's flank, and kept his boots on. At the break of day, restless as ever, he was off again. Crossing the Jimenez River in a native ferry while the horses swam, we passed through tiny villages that had not seen a white man for a year. Our journey now lay through the woods, and Skim, dismounting, stalked along the narrow trail as though he had been shod in seven-league boots. I heard a pistol shot ring out, and, coming up, found Skim in mortal combat with an ape. Then one more plunge into a river, and another stream spanned by a bamboo pole, which we negotiated like funambulists, dragging the steeds below us by their halters,—then Balingasag.

In town the big *vaquero* was a schoolboy on a holiday. He was a perfect panther for prowling around the streets at night, and in the market-place, where we now missed the scattering of khaki, he became acquainted with the natives, and drank *tuba* with them. He came back with reports about the resources of the town. There was an Indian merchant stranded at Ramon's, who had a lot of watches for sale cheap. He purchased some lace curtains at the *Chino* store, and yellow *piña* cloth for a mosquito bar, and with this stuff he had transformed his bed into a perfect bower. It was almost a contradiction that this wild fellow, who was more accustomed to his boots and spurs at night than to pajamas, should have taken so much pains to make his sleeping-quarters dainty. Streamers of baby-ribbon fell in graceful lines about the curtains, while the gauze mosquito-bar was decorated with the medals he had won for bravery.

A photograph of his divorced wife occupied the place of honor near the looking-glass. In reminiscent moods Skim used to tell how Chita, of old Mexico, had left him after stabbing him three times with the jeweled knife that he had given her. "I didn't interfere with her," he said, "but told her, when she pricked me with the little knife, it was my heart that she was jabbing at." Skim also told me of his expedition into "Dead Man's Gulch," "Death Valley," and the suddenly-abandoned mining-camps among the hills of California. And he had met the daughter of a millionaire in Frisco, and had seen her home. "And when I saw the big shack looming up there in the woods," he said, "I thought sure that I'd struck the wrong farmhouse."

Skim rented a small place surrounded by a hedge of bonga palms, and here he entertained the village royally. He was a favorite among the girls, and lavished gifts upon them, mostly the latest illustrated magazines that belonged to me. He ruled his awkward soldiers with an iron hand, and they were more afraid of him that of the Evil One. Of course, they could not understand his Spanish, and would often answer, "*Si, señor*" when they had not the least idea of what the orders were. Then they would come to grief for disobedience, or receive Skim's favorite reprimand of "Blooming idiot! *No sabe* your own language?" When his cook displeased him, he (the cook) would generally come bumping down the stairs. The voice of Skim was as the roaring lion in a storm. Desertions were many in those strenuous days; for the constabulary guards were not the heroes of the hour.

Always insisting on strict discipline, Skim, on the day we made our trial hike, marshaled his forces in a rigid line, and, after roll-call, marched them off in order to the hills. The soldiers took about three steps to his one, and, trying to keep up with him through the dense hemp-fields, they broke ranks and ran. We followed a mountain stream to its headwaters, scrambling over bowlders, wading waist-deep in the ice-cold stream, and by the time we broke the underbrush and pushed up hill, big Skim had literally hiked the soldiers off their feet. They were unspeakably relieved when we sat down at noon in the cool shade, upon the brink of a deep, crystal pool, and ate our luncheon. Skim, insisting that the canned quail— which retained its gamy flavor—was beyond redemption, turned it over to the soldiers to their great delight.

In spite of his severity, Skim had a soft heart, and when all dressed in white and gold, he would go up to visit Señor Roa and his daughters; while the girls would play duets on the piano, Skim, with a little chocolate baby under either arm, would sing in an insinuating voice one of his good old cowboy songs, regardless of the fact that he was not in tune with his accompaniment. He always appeared on Sundays cleanly shaven and immaculate in white, and when the girls went by his house to church, their dusky arms glowing among the gauze, appealed to him and made him sad.

No one could ever contradict Skim, though he couldn't even write his own name legibly. His monthly reports were actually works of art. "Seenyor Inspekter of constabulery," he would write, "i hav the honner to indite the following report. i hav bin having trubel with the moros. They was too boats of them and they had a canon in the bow. i faired three shots and too of them fell down but they al paddeled aeway so fast i coodnt catch them." And again: "On wensday the first instant i went on a hike of seven miles. i captured three ladrones four bolos, one old gun and too durks." Then after practicing his signature for half an hour on margins of books or any kind of paper he could find, he used to sign his document with a tremendous flourish.

I rather miss the rock thrown at my blinds at 4 o'clock A. M. A little catlike sergeant, a *mestizo*, is in charge of the constabulary, and the men are glad. No longer does the huge six-footer, with his army Colt's, stalk through the village streets. The other day I got a note from Skim: "i dont think i ain't never going to come back there eny moar," he wrote above the most successful signature that I had ever seen. A few months later Skim was badly crippled in a fight with robbers. He was sent to Manila to the civil hospital. On his discharge he was promoted, and he now wears three bars on his shoulder-straps. He has been shot three times since then, and he has written, "If i dont get kilt no more, i dont think that i wont come back."

To-day the constabulary is well organized. They have distinguished themselves time and again in battle-line. They have put down the lingering sparks of the rebellion. They look smart in their brand-new uniforms and russet boots. But it was only a year or two ago that Skim had crowded their uncivilized feet into the clumsy army shoe, and knocked them around like puppets in a Noah's ark. Skim, if you ever get hold of these few pages written in your honor, here's my compliments and my best wishes for another bar upon your shoulder-straps, and—yes, here's hoping that you "won't get killed no more."

II.

Last Days at Oroquieta.

I had been visiting the teachers at El Salvador, who occupied a Spanish convent, with a broad veranda looking out upon the blue sea and a grove of palms. It was a country of bare hills, which reminded one somewhat of Colorado. *Nipa* jungles bristled at the mouths of rivers, and the valleys were verdant with dense mango copses. We made our first stop on the way from Cagayan on Sunday morning at a village situated in a prairie, where a drove of native ponies had been tethered near the *nipa* church. The roads were alive with people who had been attending services or who were on the way to the next cock-fight. Falling in with a loquacious native, who supplied us with a store of mangoes, we rode on, and reached Tag-nipa or El Salvador late in the afternoon.

One of the teachers, "Teddy," might have actually stepped from out the pages of Kate Greenaway. He had a large, broad forehead, and a long, straight nose. He conducted a school of miserable little girls, and in the evening, like a village preacher, he would make his pastoral calls with a "Hello, girlie!" for each child he met. When he was pleased at anything, he used to clap his hands, exclaiming, "Goodie!" "Teddy" envied me "my baccalaureate enthusiasm," and, encouraged evidently by this quality, he would read Chaucer in a sing-song voice, or, when this recreation failed, would make up limericks to a guitar accompaniment. His partner was the one who wore the transposed leggings, and who walked as though continually following a plow.

Leaving for Oroquieta, in a Moro sailboat stocked with Chinese pigs and commissaries that belonged to one called "Jac-cook" by the natives, or "The Great White Father"—a New Zealander who could have posed as an Apollo or a Hercules—the sailors whistled for wind, and finally succeeded in obtaining it. The moon rose early over the dark waters, and the boat, behaving admirably, rode the huge waves like a cockle. We had nearly gone to pieces on a coral reef that night if "Jac-cook," suddenly aroused by the unusual sound of breakers, had not lowered sail in time to save the ship from running on the sharp rock half a mile from land. The sailors, perfectly incompetent, and panic-stricken at the course the boat was taking, blundered frightfully as the New Zealander assumed command.

No doubt the best mess in the town at that time was the one conducted by the members of the hospital detachment. "Shorty," who did the cooking, was a local druggist in his way; that is, he sold the natives talcum powder, which they bought at quinine rates. The acting steward, whom all the Filipinos called "Francisco," though his name was Louis, was a butcher, and a doctor too. Catching the Spaniard's goat out late at night, he knocked it in the head. The carcass was then taken into the dissecting-room, where it was skinned and dressed for the fresh-meat supply. He had acquired a local reputation as a *medico*, to the disgust of the real army doctor, who, for a long time, could not imagine why his medicines had disappeared so fast. Then there was "Red," who had the art of laziness down fine, and who could usually be found playing *monte* with the natives. With the money he had won at *monte* games and chicken-fights, he intended to set up a drugstore in America.

In a downpour of rain I left one morning for Aloran, down the coast and up the winding river. Prisoners furnished by the *presidente* manned the *banca*. They were guarded by a barefooted municipal policeman, who, on falling presently to sleep, would probably have lost his Mauser overboard had not one of the convicts rescued it and courteously returned it to him. It was a wet and lonesome pull up the Aloran River, walled in on both sides by *nipa* jungles, and forever winding in and out. After an hour or so, while I was wondering what we were coming to, we met a raft poled down the stream with "Red" and a young Austrian constabulary officer aboard.

Finding a little teacup of a house, I moved in, and, before an interested throng of natives, started to unpack my trunks and boxes with a sense of genuine relief; for I had had four months of traveling and living out of steamer-trunks. But I returned to Oroquieta all in good time for the doctor's birthday and the annual Oroquieta ball. I found the doctor wandering about Aloran late one afternoon; for he had been attending a sick Chinaman. We started back together through the night, and, in the darkness, voices greeted us, or snarled a "*Buenas noches*" at us as we passed. Bridges that carabaos had fallen through were crossed successfully, and we arrived at Oroquieta during the band concert.

The foreign colony at Oroquieta was more interesting than the *personæ dramatis* of the "Canterbury Tales." Where to begin I do not know. But, anyway, there was my old friend the constabulary captain, "Foxy Grandpa," as we called him then, because when he was not engaged in telling how he had arrested somebody in Arizona, he was playing practical jokes or doing tricks with cards and handkerchiefs. And then there was the "Arizona Babe," a blonde of the Southwestern type, affianced to the commissary sergeant. The wife o£ the commanding officer, a veritable O'Dowd, and little Flora, daughter of O'Dowd, who rode around town in a pony cart, were leaders of society for the subpost.

Then you could take a stool in front of Paradies's general store, and almost at any time engage the local teacher in an argument. You would expect, of course, that he would wander from his topic till you found yourself discussing something entirely foreign to the subject, but so long as he was talking, everything was satisfactory. There were the two Greek traders who had "poisoned the wells" out Lobuc way,—so people said. And I must not forget "Jac-cook," whose grandfather, according to his own report, had been a cannibal, a king of cannibals, and eaten a roast baby every morning for his breakfast. Jack was a soldier of fortune if there ever was one. He could give you a recipe for making *poi* from ripe bananas and the milk of cocoanuts, or for distilling whisky from fermented oranges,—both of which formulas I have unfortunately lost. He recommended an exclusive diet of raw fish, and in his youth he had had many a hard battle with the shark and octopus. His one regret was that there were no sharks in the Oroquieta Bay, that, diving under, he could rip with a sharp knife. "To catch the devil-fish," he used to say, "you whirl them rapidly around your arm until they get all tangled up and supine-like." And once, like Ursus, in "Quo Vadis," he had taken a young bull by the horns and broken its neck.

All members of good standing in the colony received their invitations to the birthday party. Old Vivan, the ex-horse-doctor of the *Insurrectos*, went out early in the morning to cut palms. The floor was waxed and the walls banked with green. The first to arrive was "Fresno Bill," the Cottobato trader, in a borrowed white suit and a pair of soiled shoes. Then came the bronzed Norwegian captain of the *Delapaon*, hearty and hale from twenty years of deep-sea sailing from the Java coast to Heligoland. Came Paradies, the little German trader, in his finest blacks, and chose a seat off in one corner of the room. Then "Foxy Grandpa" and the "Arizona Babe" arrived, and the old maid from Zamboanga, who, when expression failed her, would usurp the conversation with a "blab, blab, blab!" And as the serpent made for old Laocoön, so she now made for "Fresno Bill."

Half an hour more and the party was in full swing. Native musicians, stationed on the landing, furnished the music, and Vivan, the Filipino Chesterfield, with sweeping bows to every one, was serving the refreshments. Padre Pastor, in his black gown, with his face all wreathed in smiles, was trying to explain to the schoolteacher's wife that "stars were the forget-me-nots of heaven." The young commissary sergeant had secured an alcove for the "Arizona babe," and "Foxy grandpa," taking a nip of something when his good wife's back was turned, was telling his best anecdote of the southwest, "Ichabod Crane," the big-boned Kansan—who had got the better of us all that afternoon in argument—swinging his arms, and with his head thrown back, was trying to herd the people into an old-fashioned reel. Grabbing the little daughter of the regiment together with the French constabulary officer—they loved each other like two cats—he shouted, "Salamander, there! Why don't you salamander?" Entering into the fun more than the rest, the genial army doctor "kept the ball a-rolling."

For the doctor was a southerner, as many of the army people are. In his dual function of physician-soldier, he could boast that he had killed more men, had more deaths to his credit, than his fellow officers. He was undoubtedly the best leech in the world. When off duty he assumed a Japanese kimono, which became him like the robes of Nero. Placing his sandaled feet upon the window-sill, he used to read the *Army and Navy Journal* by the hour. Although he had a taste for other literature, his studies were considerably hampered by a tendency to fall asleep after the first few paragraphs. He spent about four weeks on "Majorie Daw." When he was happy—and he generally was happy—he would sing that favorite song of his, "O, Ca'line." It went:

> "O, Ca'line! O, Ca'line!
> Can't you dance da pea-vine?
> O, my Jemima, O-hi-o."

But he could never explain satisfactorily what the "pea-vine" was. His "Ring around and shake a leg, ma lady," was a triumph in the lyric line.

We used to walk to Lobuc every afternoon to purchase eggs. The doctor's "*Duna ba icao itlong dinhi?*" always amused the natives, who, when they had any eggs, took pleasure in producing them. It was with difficulty that I taught him to say "*itlog*" (egg) instead of "eclogue," which he had been using heretofore. He made one error, though, which never could be rectified,—he always called a Chinaman a "hen chick," much to the disgust of the offended Oriental, whose denomination was expressed in the Visayan by the word "*inchic*."

I pause before attempting a description of the Oroquieta ball, and, like the poets, pray to some kind muse to guide my pen. To-night I feel again the same thrill that I felt the night of the grand Oroquieta ball. The memories of Oroquieta music seem as though they might express themselves in words:

> "The stars so brightly shine,
> But ah, those stars of thine!
>   Are none like yours, *Bonita*,
> Beyond the ocean brine."

And then I seem to see the big captain—"Foxy grandpa"—beating the bass drum like that extraordinary man that Mark Twain tells about, "who hadn't a tooth in his whole head." I can remember how Don Julian, the crusty Spaniard, animated with the spirit of old Capulet, stood on the chair and shouted, "*Viva los Americanos!*"—and the palm-grove, like a room of many pillars, lighted by Chinese lanterns.

It was a time of magic moonlight, when the sea broke on the sands in phosphorescent lines in front of the *kiosko*. Far out on the horizon lights of fishing-boats would glimmer, and the dusky shores of Siquijor or the volcanic isle of Camaguin loomed in the distance. Here there were little cities as completely isolated though they were parts of another planet, where the "other" people worked and played, and promenaded to the strumming of guitars. And in the background rose the triple range of mountains, cold, mysterious, and blue in the transfiguring moonlight.

The little army girl, like some fair goddess of the night, monopolized the masculine attention at the ball. When she appeared upon the floor, all others, as by mutual consent, retired, and left the field to her alone. The "Pearls of Lobuc," who refused to come until a carriage was sent after them, appeared in delicate gauze dresses, creamy stockings, and white slippers. And "The Princess of the Philippines," Diega, with her saucy pompadour, forgot that it was time to drop your hand at the conclusion of the dance. Our noble Ichabod was there in a tight-fitting suit of black and narrow trousers, fervently discussing with the French constabulary man whether a frock was a Prince Albert. Paradies capered mincingly to the quick music of the waltz, and the old maid, unable to restrain herself, kept begging the doctor—who did not know how to dance—only to try a two-step with her, please. And the poor doctor, in his agony, had sweated out another clean white uniform. I had almost forgotten Maraquita and the *zapatillas* with the pearl rosettes. She was a little queen in pink-and-white, and ere the night was over she had given me her "*sing sing*" (ring) and fan, and told me that I could "ask papa" if I wanted to. The next day she was just as pretty in light-blue and green, and with her hair unbound. She poked her toes into a pair of gold-embroidered sandals, and seemed very much embarrassed at my presence. This was explained when, later in the day, her uncle asked me for Miss Maraquita's ring.

Although the cook and the *muchachos* ate the greater part of the refreshments, and a heart or two was broken incidentally, the Oroquieta ball passed into history as being the most brilliant function of its kind that ever had been witnessed at the post.

The winter passed with an occasional plunge in the cool river, and the surf-bath every morning before breakfast. In the evening we would ride to Lobuc, racing the ponies back to town in a white cloud of dust. Dinner was always served for any number, for we frequently had visitors,—field officers on hunting leave, commercial drummers from Cebu, the circuit judge, the captain of the *Delapaon*. The doctor had been threatening for some time, now, to give Vivan a necessary whipping, which he did one morning to that Chesterfield's astonishment. Calling the servant *"Usted,"* or "Your honor," he applied the strap, and old Vivan was shaking so with laughter that he hardly felt the blows. But after that, he tumbled over himself with eagerness to fill our orders. We had found the coolest places in the town,—the beach at Lobuc, under a wide-spreading tree, and the thatched bridge where the wind swept up and down the river, where the women beat their washing on the rounded stones, and carabaos dreamed in the shade of the bamboo. The cable used to steady the bridge connected with the shore, the doctor explained to the old maid, was the Manila cable over which the messages were sent.

The clamor of bells one morning reminded us that the *fiesta* week was on, and old Vivan came running in excitedly with the intelligence that seven *bancas* were already anchored at the river's mouth, and there were twenty more in sight. Then he went breathlessly around the town to circulate the news. We rode about in Flora's pony cart, and sometimes went to visit "Foxy Grandpa," wife, and "Arizona Babe." "Old Tom," the convict on parole for murder, waited on the table, serving the pies that Mrs. G. had taught the cook to make, and the canned peaches with evaporated cream. Then, on adjourning to the parlor, with its pillars and white walls, the "Babe" would play "Old Kentucky Home" on the piano till the china shepherdesses danced with the vibrations, and the genial captain, growing reminiscent, would recall the story of the man he had arrested in old Mexico, or even condescend to do a new trick with a handkerchief. There was a curious picture from Japan in a gilt frame that had the place of honor over the piano. It was painted on a plaque of china, robin's-egg blue, inlaid with bits of pearl,—which represented boats or something on the Inland Sea, while figures of men and small boys, enthusiastically waving Japanese flags, all cut out of paper, had been pasted on. There was an arched bridge over the blue water, and a sampan sculled by a boatman in a brown *kimono*. There was a house with paper windows and a thatched roof.

... *Chino* José died, and was given a military funeral. The bier was covered with the Stars and Stripes. A company of native scouts was detailed as an escort, and the local band led the procession to the church. Old "Ichabod," with a long face, and in a dress suit, with a purple four-in-hand tie, followed among the candle-bearers with long strides. The tapers burning in the nave resembled a small bonfire, and exhaustive masses finally resulted, so I judge, in getting the old heathen's spirit out of purgatory. Good old *Chino* José! He had left his widow fifty thousand "Mex," of which the priest received his share; also the doctor, for the hypodermic injections of the past three months.

Then came the wedding of Bazon, whose bride, for her rebellious love, had recently been driven from her mother's home. Bazon, touched by this act of loyalty, cut his engagement with another girl and made the preparations for the wedding feast. I met the little Maraquita at Bazon's reception, and conversed with her through an interpreter. "The *señorita* says," so the interpreter informed me, "she appreciates your conversation very much, and thinks you play the piano very well. She has a new piano in her house that came from Paris. In a little while the *señorita* will depart for Spain, where she intends to study in a convent for a year." Ah, Maraquita! She had had an *Insurrecto* general for a suitor, and had turned him down. And she had jilted Joe, the French constabulary officer, and had rejected a neighboring merchant's offer for her hand of fifty carabaos. I have to-day a small reminder of her dainty needlework—a family of Visayan dolls which she had dressed according to the native mode.

One day the undertaker's boat dropped in with a detachment of the burial corps aboard. The bodies of the soldiers that had slept for so long in the convent garden were removed, and taken in brass caskets back across the sea....

We started out one morning on constabulary ponies, brilliantly caparisoned in scarlet blankets and new saddles. "Ichabod," the Kansas *maestro*, had proposed to guide us to Misamis over the mountain trail. It was not long, however, before one spoke of trails in the past tense. The last place that was on the map—a town of questionable loyalty, that we had gladly left late in the afternoon—now seemed, as we remembered it, in contrast with the wilderness, a small metropolis. The Kansan still insisted that he was not lost. "Do you know where we are?" I asked. "Wa-al," he replied, "those mountains ought to be 'way over on the other side of us, and the flat side of the moon ought to be turned the other way." We wandered for ten hours through prairies of tall buffalo-grass, at last discovering a trail that led down to the sea. The ponies were as stiff as though they had been made of wood instead of flesh and blood.

We had Thanksgiving dinner at the doctor's. Old Tom did the cooking, and Vivan, all smiles, waited upon the guests. Stuffed chicken and roast sucking pig, and a young kid that the *muchachos* had tortured to death that morning, sawing its throat with a dull knife, were the main courses. Padre Pastor, who had held a special mass that morning for Americans, "returned thanks," rolling his eyes, and saying something about the flowers not being plentiful or fragrant, but the stars, exceptional in brilliance, compensating for the floral scantiness. The doctor sang "O, Ca'line," and the captain did tricks with the napkins. Everybody voted this Thanksgiving a success.

The weary days that followed at Aloran were relieved late in December by a visit from the doctor, and a new constabulary officer named Johnson,1 who had ridden out on muddy roads, through swimming rice-pads, across swollen rivers. When the store of commissaries was exhausted, we rode back, and Johnson came to grief by falling through an open bridge into a rice-swamp, so that all that we could see of him was a square inch of his poor horse's nose. We pulled him out, and named the place "Johnson's Despair."

Our Christmas Eve was an eventful one. The transport *Trenton* went to pieces on our coral reef. We were expecting company, and when the boat pulled in, we went down to the beach to tell them where the landing was. "We thought that you were trying to tell us we were on a rock," the little cavalry lieutenant, who had been at work all night upon the pumps, said, when we saw him in the morning. It was like a shipwreck in a comic opera, so easily the vessel grounded; and at noon the next day we were invited out on shipboard for a farewell luncheon. The boat was listed dangerously to port, and, as the waves rolled in, kept bumping heavily upon the coral floor. The hull under the engines was staved in, and, as the tide increased, the vessel twisted as though flexible. Broken amidships, finally, she twisted like some tortured creature of the deep. The masts and smokestacks branched off at divergent angles, giving the ship a rather drunken aspect. At high tide the masts and deck-house were swept off; the bow went, and the boat collapsed and bent. By evening nothing was left except the bowsprit rocking defiantly among the breakers, a broken skeleton, the keel and ribs, and the big boiler tumbling and squirting in the surf.

There were three shipwrecked mariners to care for,—the bluff captain, one of nature's noblemen, who had spent his life before the mast and on the bridge, and who had been tossed upon many a strange and hostile coast. He had a deep scar on his head, received when he was shanghaied twenty years before. He told strange stories of barbaric women dressed in sea-shells; of the Pitcairn islanders, who formerly wore clothes of papyrus, but now dressed in the latest English fashion, trading the native fruits and melons for the merchandise of passing ships.

Then there was Mac, the chief, a stunted, sandy little man, covered with freckles, and tattooed with various marine designs. He loved his engine better than himself, and in his sorrow at its break-up, he was driven to the bottle, and when last seen—after asking "ever' one" to take a drink—was wandering off, his arms around two Filipino sailors. Coming to life a few days later, "Mac ain't sayin' much," he said, "but Mac, 'e knows." Yielding to our persuasion, he wrote down a song "what 'e 'ad learned once at a sailors' boardin' 'ouse in Frisco." It was called "The Lodger," and he rendered it thus, in a deep-sea voice:

> "The other night I chanced to meet a charmer of a girl,
>   An', nothin' else to do, I saw 'er 'ome;
> We 'ad a little bottle of the very finest brand,
>   An' drank each other's 'ealth in crystal foam.
> I lent the dear a sover'ign; she thanked me for the same
>   An' laid 'er golden 'ead upon me breast;
> But soon I finds myself thrown out the passage like shot,—
> A six-foot man confronts me, an' 'e says:

CHORUS—

> I'm sorry to disturb you, but the lodger 'as come," etc.

The feature of the song, however, was Mac's leer, which, in a public hall, would have brought down the house, and which I feel unable to describe.

The mate, aroused by the example of the chief, rendered a "Tops'l halliard shanty," "Blow, Bullies, Blow." It was almost as though a character had stepped from *Pinafore*, when the athletic, gallant little mate, giving a hitch to his trousers, thus began: "Strike up a light there, Bullies; who's the last man sober?" SONG.

> "O, a Yankee ship came down the river —
>   Blow, Bullies, blow!
> Her sails were silk and her yards were silver —
>   Blow, my Bully boys, blow!
> Now, who do you think was the cap'n of 'er?
>   Blow, Bullies, blow!
> Old Black Ben, the down-east bucko —
>   Blow, my Bully boys, How!"

"'Ere is a shanty what the packeteers sings when, with 'full an' plenty,' we are 'omeward bound. It is a 'windlass shanty,' an' we sings it to the music of the winch. The order comes 'hup anchors,' and the A one packeteer starts hup:

> "'We're hom'ard bound; we're bound away;
>   Good-bye, fare y' well.
> We're home'ard bound; we leave to-day;
>   Hooray, my boys! we're home'ard bound.
> We're home'ard bound from Liverpool town;
>   Hooray, my boys, hooray!
> A bully ship and a bully crew;
>   Good-bye, fare y' well.
> A bucko mate an' a skipper too;
>   Hooray, my boys, we're home'ard bound!'"

For the old maid this was the time the ages had been waiting for. What anxious nights she spent upon her pillow or before the looking-glass; what former triumphs she reviewed; and what plans for the conquest she had made, shall still remain unwritten history. When she was ready to appear, we used to hear her nervous call, "Doctor! Can I come over?" Poor old maid! She couldn't even wait till she was asked. How patiently she stirred the hot tomato soy the captain made; O yes! She could be useful and domestic. How tenderly she leaned upon the arm of the captain's chair, caressing the scar upon his head "where he was shanghaied!" Then, like Othello, he would entertain her with his story about the ladies in the sea-shell clothes, or of the time when he had "weathered the Horn" in a "sou'wester." She was flurried and excited all the week. The climax came after the captain left for Iligan. The old maid learned somehow that he was going to Manila on a transport which would pass by Oroquieta but a few miles out. Sending a telegram to the chief quartermaster whom she called a "dear," she said that if the ship would stop to let her on, she could go out to meet it in a *banca*. Though the schoolmaster and his wife had also requested transportation on the same boat, the old maid, evidently thinking that "three made a crowd," wired to her friend the quartermaster not to take them on.

We met the old maid almost in hysterics on the road to Lobuc. "O, for the love of God!" she cried, "get me a boat, and get my trunk down to the shore. I have about ten minutes left to catch that ship." It was old Ichabod who rowed her out in the canoe—the old maid, with the sun now broken out behind the clouds, her striped parasol, and a small steamer trunk. It was a mad race for old Ichabod, and they were pretty well drenched when the old maid climbed aboard the transport, breathless but triumphant. I have since learned that Dido won her wandering Æneas in Manila, and that the captain finally has found his "bucko mate."

It was old Ichabod's delight to teach a class of sorry-looking *señoritas*, with their dusty toes stuck into carpet slippers, and their hair combed back severely on their heads. The afternoons he spent in visiting his flock; we could descry him from afar, chin in the air, arms swinging, hiking along with five-foot strides. If he could "doctor up" the natives he was satisfied. He knew them all by name down to the smallest girl, and he applied his healing lotions with the greatest sense of duty, much to the amusement of the regular M.D. But Ichabod was qualified, for he had once confided to me that at one time he had learned the names of all the bones in the left hand!

The colony showed signs of breaking up. The native scouts had gone, leaving their weeping *"hindais"* on the shore. "Major O'Dowd," his wife, and Flora had also departed to a station *sin Americanos* up in the interior. At this, the doctor, for the first time in his life, broke into song, after the style and meter of immortal Omar:

> "Hiram, indeed is gone; his little Rose
> Vamosed to Lintogoup with all her clothes;
> > But still the Pearls are with us down the line,
> And many a *hindai* to the *tubig* goes."

"Tubig," he said, "did not mean 'water.' It was more poetical, expressing the idea of fountain, watering-place, or spa."

It was my last day at Aloran. In the morning I ascended a near elevation, and looked down upon the sleepy valley spread below. There was the river winding in and out; there was the convent, like a doll-house in a field of green. Vivan had gone on with the trunks and boxes packed upon a carabao. The ponies were waiting in the compound. Valedictories were quickly said; but there was little Peter with his silken cheeks, the brightest little fellow I have ever known. It seemed a shame to leave him there in darkest Mindanao. Turning the horses into the Aloran River at the ford we struck the high road near the *barrio* of Feliz. Galloping on, past "Columbine" bridge, "Skeleton" bridge, "Johnson's Despair," and Fenis, we arrived at Oroquieta in good time.

But what a change from the old place as we had known it! Hiram, indeed was gone. The doctor had set out for pastures new. The "Arizona Babe" and "Foxy Grandpa" had departed for fresh fields. Like one who, falling asleep in a theater, awakes to find the curtain down and the spectators gone, so I now looked about the vacant town. The actors had departed, and "the play was played out."

Footnote:

1 Johnson, the runaway constabulary officer, was killed October last by the crew of the native boat which he had captured after the Steamship "Victoria," which he had seized, had grounded off

the coast of Negros. Four of the crew were killed during the fight. In true brigand style he had taken the boat at the revolver's point, and headed for the coast of Borneo. He had ten thousand dollars of government money, and his intention was to land at various ports and make the local merchants "stand and deliver." I gave the following interview to the reporter of the Princeton (Indiana) "Clarion-News," October 16, 1903:

"'Johnson, the pirate,' is dead, and buried in the lonely isle of Negros. Many a worse man occupies a better grave. The worst that you can say of Johnson is, that he was wrong and that he liked to drink too much.

"I shall always remember him in his red shoulder straps, his khaki riding suit and leather leggings. Before I had ever seen him I had heard the old constabulary captain say: 'That feller looks like a born fighter. Bet he ain't afraid of anything.' ... The padre gave us a Christmas dinner, and Johnson at this function took too much of the communion wine. On the way back he reeled continually in his saddle, vomiting a stream of red wine....

"We often used to race our ponies into Oroquieta neck and neck, scattering natives, chickens, and pigs to right and left. The last I saw of him was as he put out on a stormy sea in a frail Moro sailboat bound for Cagayan, which at that time was infested with ladrones.

"Johnson was only a boy, but he had been a sailor and a soldier, and had seen adventures in the Canary Islands, in Cuba, and the Philippines. The boat that he held up and started off to Borneo was one employed in questionable trade. She was a smuggler, and had formerly been in the service of the 'Insurrecto' Government. She used to drop in at a port at night and pull out in the morning with neither a bill of lading nor a manifest.

"Johnson should not be blamed too much for the wild escapade. The climate had undoubtedly affected him; moreover the constabulary has no business putting heavy responsibilities upon young boys."

Chapter XIII.
In Camp and Barracks with the Officers and Soldiers of the Philippines.

Bugle-calls, loud, strident bugle-calls, leaping in unison from the brass throats of bugles; tawny soldiers lining up for guard-mount before the officer of the day, as spick and span as a toy soldier; troopers in blue shirts, with their mess-kits in their hands, running across the street for rations; men in khaki everywhere, raising a racket on pay-day, fraternizing with the Filipinos when off duty; poker games in the barracks, with the army cot and blanket for a table; taps, and the measured tread of sentries, and anon a startled challenge, "Halt! Who's there?"—such were the days in Cagayan in 1901.

The blue sea, stretching out into the hazy distance, sparkled around the little *nipa*-covered dock where commissary stores and sacks of rice were piled. The native women, squatting on the ground, were selling mangoes and bananas to the boys. "Cagayan Mag," who vended the hot bottled beer for "jawbone," digging her toes into the dust, was entertaining the surrounding crowd with her coarse witticisms. The corporal of the guard, reclining in an easy steamer-chair, under his tent extension, was perusing the news columns from the States, by this time three months old. A sunburnt soldier, with his Krag upon his shoulder, paced the dock, wearily doing the last hour of his guard.

"Do you-all like hawg-jowl and black-eyed peas?" drawled "Tennessee Bill," shifting his bony form to a more comfortable position on the rice-sack.

"Reckon I ort ter; I wuz bo'n in Geo'gy," said his comrade, as he rolled a rice-straw paper cigarette.

After an interval of several minutes the same conversation was repeated. Suddenly a sharp toot sent the echoes scudding back and forth among the hills. A moment later the small transport, with the usual blur of khaki in her bows, came swinging around the promontory.

"Pshaw! I thought it wuz the pay boat comin'" grumbled Bill.

Then, as the *Trenton* pulled up to the dock, signs of activity began to animate that place. The guard, with leveled bayonet, began to shoo the "Gugus" off the landing. Down the hot road, invested in a cloud of dust, an ambulance was coming, drawn by a team of army mules and bringing the lieutenant quartermaster and his sergeants.

"Why, hello!" said Bill; "if here ain't little Wantz a-comin'. Got his discharge an' gone married a *babay*."

The soldiers crowded around the ex-hospital corps man, who, still in his khaki suit, was standing on the shore with a sad-looking Filipino girl in tow. Her feet were bare and dusty, and she wore a turkey-red skirt caught up on one side, and a gauze *camisa* with a *piña* yoke, and the stiff, flaring sleeves. Her head was bare, and her black hair was combed uncompromisingly back on her head. Her worldly goods were done up in a straw mat and a soiled bandana handkerchief, and were deposited before her on the ground.

"This is the gal," said Wantz; "old Justice de Laguna's daughter, and the same what uster sell beer to the Twenty-eighth over at Tagaloan. She ain't no beauty, but she's a good steady trotter; ain't you, Dell?" The girl looked stupid and embarrassed, and did not reply.

A "rooky," who had joined the company, stood on the dock disconsolately. His blanket roll and locker had been put off the boat. This was his first appearance in the provinces. He was a stranger in a strange land, a fish out of water, and a raw recruit.

The men were set to work immediately landing the commissary stores. They stripped their shoes and socks off, rolled up their trousers to the knee, and waded through the shallow water, carrying the bales and boxes on their shoulders to the shore.

The road up to the town was lined with *nipa* houses, shaded with banana-trees and bonga palms. This was the road that was almost impassable during the rainy season. As the ambulance rolled heavily along, scores of half-naked babies, shaped like peanuts, shouted after you a "Hello, baby!" and the pigs, with snouts like coal-scuttles, scattered on either side the thoroughfare. This was the famous "Bolo alley," down which, only a few months before, the *Insurrecto* army had come shouting, "*A la! á la!*" firing as they ran.

You passed the market-place, an open hall filled with the native stalls, where soldiers loafed around, chatting with the Visayan girls—for a freemasonry exists between the Filipino and the soldier—dickering with one for a few dhobie cigarettes, sold "jawbone," to be paid for when the pay-boat comes.

The troops were quartered in old Spanish buildings, where the sliding windows of the upper floors disclosed the lanes of white mosquito-bar. Back in the courtyard, where the cook was busily preparing mess, a mangy and round-shouldered monkey from the bamboo fence was looking on approvingly. The cook was not in a good humor. All that the mess had had for three weeks was the regulation beans and bacon, without a taste of fresh meat or fresh vegetables.

Things were as bad, however, at the officers' mess, where the rule was that the first complaint should sentence its author to conduct the mess himself until relieved in a like manner. As might be imagined, such a system naturally discouraged an improvement of affairs. Exasperated, finally, beyond his limit, Lieutenant Breck came out with—"If this isn't the rottenest apology of an old mess"—saving himself by quickly adding, "But I like it; O, I like it; nobody can tell how much I like this mess!"

There was an officer's club in a frame building near the headquarters. Here, in the afternoon, the clan would gather for a round of "whisky poker" for the drinks. There was a strapping young Kentuckian whose ancestors had all been army men. "The profession of arms," said he, "is the noblest profession in the world. And that is the profession that we follow." It was a rather sad sight, though, a few weeks later, after his wife, a little Southern girl, had gone back to the "States," to see this giant soldier playing cards and drinking whisky with the teamsters, bar-keeps, and camp-followers, threatening to shoot the man who tried to interfere, and finally being taken down in irons for a court-martial.

The only one of all his friends who did not fall away from him was one, a little, catlike cavalry lieutenant, booted and spurred, and always dressed in khaki riding-breeches, never saying much, but generally considered the most popular young officer in all the service. And there was one other faithful one, but not an officer. The "striker," who had followed him in many a hard hike, and had learned to admire his courage and to consider him infallible, tried for the sake of the young Southern girl, to keep his master from the wretched drink.

The post of Cagayan that winter was a busy one. On Sunday mornings the stern-visaged officers would go the round of all the barracks on inspection duty. There was still a remnant of the *Insurrecto* army operating in the hills, and an attack upon the town was threatened nightly. Once a month, when pay-day came around, a reign of terror, which began with early afternoon, lasted until almost a company of miscellaneous marauders could have been recruited from the guard-house. A dozen saloons and poker games were running the night long, and in those days little money was deposited in the paymaster's bank.

A number of detachments had been left in different towns around the bay in charge of second lieutenants or first sergeants. Here, while the discipline was more relaxed, the pandemonium of pay-day was avoided. But the two best poker-players in the company corraling all the money, either would proceed to narrow the financial distribution further, or would shake hands and agree to make deposits on the next disbursing-day. Some of the men on their discharge would have a thousand dollars, or enough to set them up in business in the States.

These "outfits" differ greatly in their character. Some are composed of sociable, kind-hearted fellows, while others may contain a large percentage of professional "bad men" and rowdies. Each company will have its own traditions and a reputation which is guarded jealously. There was the "fighting Twenty-eighth," the regiment invincible. The soldiers grow attached to their outfit. On their discharge, which they have eagerly looked forward to, after a day or two of Frisco, when the money has been spent to the last dollar of the "finals," more than one chop-fallen soldier, looking up the first recruiting sergeant, will "take on" again.

The "company fund" is a great institution, and an "outfit" with a good fund is considered prosperous. This money goes for extras at the table, for baseball equipments, or for company mascots. The sergeant-major usually has charge of this disbursement, and the soldiers, though they grumble at his orders, can not help respecting him. The sergeant-major has been seasoned in the service. He is a ripe old fellow, and a warrior to the core. The company cook is also an important personage. It was the old cook at Balingasag—I think that he had served for twenty years—who fed me in the convent courtyard on *camotes*, egg-plant, and a chicken which he had stolen from a native. According to his theory, a soldier was a licensed robber, and the chicken should be classed as forage—not as plunder. He was a favorite among the officers, who used to get him started on his favorite grievance,—the condemnation by a board of survey of a certain army mule. "I liked that mule," he used to say. "He was the best mule that the service ever had."

The nightly "argument," or "chewing the rag," is a favorite pastime in an isolated camp. Sitting around upon the army cots or chests, the soldiers will discuss some unimportant topic until "taps" sounds.

I will admit that "Company M" was a disreputable lot. They never dressed up; frequently they went without their footgear; and they drank much *tuba* with the natives. They took delight in teaching the small boys profanity, and they would shock the Filipinos by omitting bathing-suits when in the surf. They used to frighten the poor "niggers" half to death by trying to break through their houses on a dark night. Yet I believe that every Filipino was the soldier's friend, and I am sure I noticed not a few heart-broken *señoritas* gathered at the shore when they departed. For my own part, I have always found the soldier generous, respectful, and polite.

There was a great wag in the company, who, in some former walk of life, had figured as a circus clown. He also claimed to have been upon the stage in vaudeville. He had enlisted in the regimental band, but, through some change, had come to be bugler of M Company. He owned a mandolin, called the "potato bug"—a name suggested by the inlaid bowl. He had brought back to life a cracked guitar, which he had strung with copper wire obtained by "jawbone" at the *Chino* store. It was an inspiration when he sang to the guitar accompaniment, "Ma Filipino Babe," or in a rich and melancholy voice, with the professional innuendo, "just to jolly the game along," a song entitled "Little Rosewood Casket."

It is a sorry company that doesn't number in its roll a poet. Company M had a good poet. Local customs and the local atmosphere appealed to him, and he has thus recorded his impression of the Philippines:

> "There once was a Philippine *hombre*;
> Ate *guinimos*, rice, and *legombre*;
>   His pants they were wide,
>   And his shirt hung outside;
> But this, you must know, is *costombre*.
>
> He lived in a *nipa balay*
> That served as a stable and sty.
>   He slept on a mat
>   With the dog and the cat,
> And the rest of the family near by.
>
> He once owned a *bueno manoc*,
> With a haughty and valorous look,
>   Who lost him amain
>   And *mil pesos tambien*,
>   And now he plays *monté* for luck.

This poem was received so favorably that the following effort of the realistic school escaped:

> "In this land of dhobie dreams,
>   Happy, smiling Philippines,
> Where the bolo man is hiking all day long,
> Where the natives steal and lie,
>   And *Americanos* die,
>   The soldier sings his evening song.

> Social wants are small and few;
>   All the ladies smoke and chew,
> And do other things they ought to know are wrong.
>   *Presidentes* cut no ice,
>   For they live on fish and rice,
> And the soldier sings his evening song."

There is another stanza, but the song about the "Brown Tagalog Girl" demands attention:

> "I've a *babay*, in a *balay*,
> Down in the province of Rizal.
> She's nice and neat, dainty and sweet;
> She's ma little brown Tagalog gal."

The army officers and their families still form the aristocracy of the Philippines. While army life is not all like Camp Wallace and the gay Luneta, in the larger posts throughout the provinces, both the officers and soldiers are housed very comfortably. The clubhouse down at Zamboanga has a pavilion running out over the water, where the ladies sit at night, or where refreshments are served after the concert by the band. Although their ways are not the ways of the civilian; although to them the possibilities of Jones's promotion from the bottom of the list seems of a paramount importance, you will not find anywhere so loyal and hospitable a class of people as the army officers. Whatever little jealousies they entertain among themselves are overshadowed by the fact that "he" or "she" is of the "service." And the soldiers, rough as they are, and slovenly compared to the red-coated soldiers of Great Britain, or the gray-coated troopers of the German army, are beyond doubt the finest fighting men in all the world.

Chapter XIV.
Padre Pedro, Recoleto Priest.—The Routine of a Friar in the Philippines.

It might have been the dawn of the first day in Eden. I was awakened by the music of the birds and sunlight streaming through the convent window. Heavily the broad leaves of *abacá* drooped with the morning dew. Only the roofs of a few *nipa* houses could be seen. The *tolo*-trees, like Japanese pagodas, stretched their horizontal arms against the sky. The mountains were as fresh and green as though a storm had swept them and cleared off again. They now seemed magnified in the transparent air.

All in the silence of the morning I went down to where the tropical river glided between primeval banks and under the thick-plated overhanging foliage. The water was as placid as a sheet of glass. A spirit of mystery seemed brooding near. As yet the sun's rays had not penetrated through the canopy of leaves. A lonely fisherman sat on the bank above, lost in his dreams. Down by the ford a native woman came to draw water in a bamboo tube. I half expected her to place a lighted taper on a tiny float, and send it spinning down the stream, as is the custom of the maidens on the sacred river Ganges. In the silence of the morning, in the heart of nature, thousands of miles away from telegraphs and railroads, where the brilliant-feathered birds dipped lightly into the unruffled stream, the place seemed like a sanctuary, a holy of holies, pure, immaculate, and undefiled.

The padre had arisen at six. At his command the sacristans ascended the bell-tower and proceeded to arouse the town. The padre moved about his dark, bare room. Rare Latin books were scattered around the floor. His richly embroidered vestments hung on a long line. The room was cluttered with the lumber of old crucifixes, broken images of saints, and gilded floats, considerably battered, with the candlesticks awry. The floor and the walls were bare. There was a large box of provisions in the corner, filled with imported sausages done up in tinfoil, bottles of sugar, tightly sealed to keep the ants from getting in, small cakes of Spanish chocolate, bottles of of olives and of rich communion wine. Donning his white robe, he went out to the ante-room, where, on the table spread with a white napkin, stood a cup of chocolate and a package of *La Hebra* cigarettes.

There was a scamper of bare feet as the whole force of dirty house-boys, sacristans, and cooks rushed in to kneel and kiss the padre's hand and to receive his blessing. When he had finished the thick chocolate, one of the boys brought in a glass of water, fresh and sparkling from a near-by mountain stream. Then Padre Pedro lighted his cigarette, and read in private for a little while before the morning mass began. Along the narrow pathway (for there were no streets) a string of women in black veils was slowly coming to the church. Stopping before the door, they bowed and made the sign of the cross. Then they went in and knelt down on the hard tiles. The padre's full voice, rising and falling with the chant, flooded the gloomy interior, where pencils of sunlight slanted through the apertures of the unfinished wall, and fell upon the drowsy wilderness outside.

The Oldest Cathedral of Manila

Returning from the mass, the padre refreshed himself with a small glass of gin-and-water, as his custom was; nor could the appeal of any one persuade him to take more than a single glass or to take that at an earlier or later hour. The ancient *maestra* had arrived—a wrinkled old body in a black dress and black carpet-slippers—and she knelt down to touch the padre's outstretched hand with her thin, withered lips. The little children, who were waiting for their classes to be called, all followed her example, and before long, the monotonous drone of the recitations left no doubt that school had actually begun. Benches had filled up, and the dusky feet were swinging under them as the small backs bent over knotty problems on the slates.

The padre, passing among the pupils, made the necessary erasures and corrections, and occasionally gave unasked to some recalcitrant a smart snap on the head. The morning session ended by the pupils lining up in a half circle around the battered figure of a saint—the altar decorated with red paper flowers, or colored grasses in a number of empty beer-bottles—and, while the padre played the wheezy harmonium, singing their repertoire of sacred songs. Then, as the children departed with the *"Buenos dias, señor,"* visitors, who had been waiting on the stairway with their presents of eggs, chickens, and bananas, were received.

"Thees man," the padre explained to me, as a grotesque old fellow humbled himself before us, "leeves in one house near from ze shore. He has presented me with some goud rope to tie my horses with (*buen piece, hombre*), and he says that there are no more fishes in ze sea."

"See, they have brought so many breads and fruits! They know well that eet ees my fast-day, and that my custom ees to eat no meat. I can eat fish or cheecken, but not fish *and* cheecken; eet ees difficult here to find enough food to sustain ze life on days of fast."

"Thees girl," he said, "loves me too much. She is my orphan, she and her two brothers. I have bought one house for them near from ze church, and, for the girl, one sewing-machine. Their mother had been stealed [robbed] of everything, and she had died a month ago. Ze cheeldren now have nobody but me."

She was a bright young girl, well-dressed and plump, although, when Padre Pedro had received her, she was wasted by the fever, and near starved to death. But this was only one of his many charities. He used to loan out money to the people, knowing well that they would never be able to return it. He had cured the sick, and had distributed quinine among families that could not have secured it otherwise. He went to visit his parishioners, although they had no means of entertaining him. Most of them even had no chairs for him to sit on when he came, and they would stand around in such embarrassed silence that the padre could not have derived much pleasure from their company.

At the padre's "*áver, bata!*" after the last visitor has gone, the house-boys run in with the noon meal. The padre had a good cook, who understood the art of fixing the provisions in the Spanish style. I was surprised at the resources of the parish; for a meal of ten or fifteen courses was the usual thing. A phalanx of barefooted waiters stood in line to take the plates when we had finished the respective courses, broth, mutton stew, and chicken, and bananas for dessert. The padre, I am sorry to say, ate with his knife, and was inclined to gobble. Two yellow dogs and a lean cat stood by to gulp the morsels that were thrown them from the table. When the dinner was completed, a large tumbler of water and a toothpick were brought on. After a smoke the padre took his customary nap, retiring to the low, cane-bottomed bed, where he intrenched himself behind mosquito-bars.

The convent was a rambling building, with adobe walls. It was raised up on pillars as long as telegraph poles, and the ground floor was divided into various apartments. There was the "*calaboos,*" where Padre Pedro's chickens were encouraged to "put" eggs. There were the stables for the padre's ponies, and a large bamboo stockade for pigs and chickens. The little friar took a lively interest in this corral, and he would feed his stock with his own hand from the convent window. "Ze leetle goat," he said, "eet ees my mind to send to Father Cipriano for a geeft." The sucking pig was being saved for Easter-time, when it should be well roasted on a spit, with a banana in its mouth. There were just sixty-seven chickens, and the padre used to count them every day and notice their peculiarities.

During the afternoon the padre's time was taken up by various religious duties, and the school was left in charge of the old *maestra*.

There would be a funeral service at the church, or a baptism, or confession. Some days he would be called away to other *barrios* to hear a last confession; but the distance or the weather never daunted him, and he would tuck his gown well up, and, followed by a sacristan, ride merrily away. On his return a cup of pasty chocolate would await him. Padre Pedro used to make a certain egg-fizz which was a refreshing drink of a long afternoon. The eggs were lashed into a froth by means of a bamboo brush twisted or rolled between the palms. The beauty of this beverage was that you could drain the cup, and, like the miracle of loaves and fishes, stir the batter up again, and have another drink of the same quality. "When Padre Cipriano comes here," said the friar, "eet ees very gay. Ah! Cipriano, he can make the foam come up three times. He knows well how to make thees drink."

When he would take his ebony cane and go out walking about sunset, followed by his yellow dog, the village people, young and old, would tumble over each other in their eagerness to kiss the father's hand. He would mischievously tweak the noses of the little ones, or pat the tiny girls upon the head. The friend of the lowly, he had somehow incensed the upper ten. But he had shown his nerve one Sunday morning when he had talked down one of these braggadocios who had leveled a revolver at him in the church.

The little padre was as brave as he was "game." He was a fearless rider, and there were few afternoons when we were not astride the ponies, leaping the streams and ditches in the rice-pads, swimming the fords, and racing along the beach, and it was always the little priest that set the pace. One evening he received a message from the father superior of that vicinity, old Padre José, living ten or fifteen miles up the road in an unpacified community. The notice was imperative, and only said to "come immediately, and as soon as possible."

Padre José was eighty years old, and he had been in Mindanao nearly all his life. He spoke Visayan better than the natives, and he understood the Filipinos just as though each one of them had been his child. He had been all around the island and among the pagan tribes who saw their spirits in the trees and streams. He had been back to Spain just once, and he had frozen his fingers over there. As I remember him, he was a dear, grandmotherly old fellow, in a long black gown, who bustled around so for us (we had stopped there on a certain expedition), cooking the eggs himself, and cutting the tough bologna, holding the glass of *moscatel* so lovingly up to the light before he offered it, that I almost expected him to bring forth crullers, tea, and elderberry pie. His convent was at that time occupied by the municipal authorities; and so he lived in a small *nipa* house with his two dogs, his Latin library, and the sacristans who at night slept scattered about the floor. The local conditions were unsettled at this time. The garrison at Surigao had been attacked by the so-called ladrones. Night messages were flying to and fro. Padre José's summons seemed a harbinger of trouble. But, in spite of the fact that Padre Pedro had been sick for several days, he obeyed the command of his superior like any soldier, and at midnight saddled the ponies, tucked a revolver under his gown, and started at a gallop down the road. When he arrived at Father José's house, nothing serious was found to be the matter. Only the dear old soul was lonesome and had wanted company.

Often at evening we would sit on the veranda till the evening star appeared—"the star that the shepherds know well; the precurser of the moon"—and then the angelus would ring, and Padre Pedro would stand up and doff his cap, and, after a moment spent in silent prayer, "That is good-night,'" he used to say, and then we would go in for dinner. Dinner was served at eight o'clock, and was as formal an affair as the noon meal. The evening would be spent at study, for the padre was a scholar of no mean ability. He had translated some of Stockton's stories into the Visayan language. Speaking of Stockton, Padre Pedro said that he "knew well the spirit of your countrymen." His work was frequently disturbed by the *muchachos* running in with sums that they had finished on their slates; but the padre never showed the least impatience at these interruptions.

Sometimes the "musickers" would come, and, crowding around the little organ, practice the chants for some *fiesta* day. The principal "musicker" was a grotesque old fellow, with enormous feet, and glasses rimmed with tortoise-shell. He looked so wise when he was poring over the manuscript in the dim candle-light that he reminded one of an intelligent gorilla. One of his assistants, meanwhile, would be making artificial flowers, which were to decorate the battered floats to be used in the festival procession on the morrow, carried aloft upon the shoulders of the men, sparkling with lighted tapers, while the bells up in the tower would jangle furiously. Or there would be a conference with his secretary in regard to the town records, which that functionary kept in the big book.

One night the padre was called out to attend one who, as was explained to me, was bitten by a "fool" dog. On entering the poorly-lighted shack, we found, surrounded by a gaping crowd, the victim foaming at the mouth. He had indeed been bitten by a "fool" dog, and he died a few hours afterwards, as we could do but little to relieve his suffering.

We spent the remainder of the evening looking over the long mass for Easter Sunday. And the padre said naïvely, "Will it not be necessary that I take one beer when I have reached this place, and then I can continue with the mass?" He looked back fondly to the days when he had sung his part in the antiphony in the magnificent cathedral at Manila.

The town was always at the friar's service. And no wonder! Had he not sent all the way to Manila for a Christmas box of goodies for the schoolboys,—figs, and raisins, and preserves? I caught him gloating over them one evening—when he gave his famous supper of roast kid and frosted cake for his American guests from the army post— and he had offered us a taste of these almost forgotten luxuries. How he anticipated the delight he had in store for all the boys! Then in the time of cholera, when the disease invaded even the convent, although a young man, Padre Pedro never left his post.

The only time I ever knew him to complain was when the people came in hundreds to confession. The confession-box was too hot, and the breath of the penitents offensive. "Eet ees a work of charity," he said; "they pay me nothing—nothing." The priest was only human when he feigned the toothache in order to secure a transfer to Cebu. The little station in the wilderness was too monotonous. He packed his effects in secret, fearing that the people would discover his intention and detain him. The father superior had granted him a leave of absence. His suspicions had not been aroused. When he had reached Cebu the *freile* would be under different authority, and it was even possible that he be stationed in Manila or returned to Spain. He had not seen his parents for ten years, but his education had prepared him for a life of sacrifice. For the first time he felt neglected and forgotten. On arriving at the trading port, he learned that his parishioners had found him out. They sent a delegation to entreat him to remain. The little padre's heart was touched. "They love me too much," he said, "and they have nobody but me."

My friend the padre might have been an exception to the general rule. He was a "Friar in the Philippines," a member of a much-maligned religious order. Still I have met a number of their priests and bishops, and have found them charming and delightful men. They are such hospitable entertainers that they have been frequently imposed upon by traveling Americans, who take the convents for hotels, regardless of the public sentiment. It was the friars of San Augustin who, in 1565, subdued and pacified the Cebuanos when the arms of Spain availed but little. It was the *Freile* Pedro de San Augustin, the "fighting padre," who, in 1639, defeated the lake Moros. And, in 1754, a Spanish *freile*, Father Ducos, commanding the fleet of Iligan, defeated the armada of the Moro pirates, killing about a thousand of these buccaneers.

Of course there have been friars good and bad. But "Father Peter," though he might have had good cause to dislike the Americans, had always expressed the greatest admiration for them. They were "political" (diplomatic) men. His mastering the English language was a compliment to us such as few Spaniards have seen fit to pay. He might have been narrow in religious matters, but, above all, he was conscientious. While he could bathe his hands or face in the Aloran River, he could not go in. His education was a Spartan one, and narrowing in its influences. All the society that he had ever had was that of a hundred students with the same ideals and inclinations as his own. The reputation of the friars in the Philippines has been depreciated by the conduct of the native priests. There was a padre named Pastor, an arrant coward, and wholly ignorant and superstitious. Sly old fox, he used to bet his last cent on the cock-fights, hiding up in the back window of Don Julian's. Once, on a drunken spree, he let a layman wear his gown and rosary. The natives, showing more respect for the sacred vestments than the priest had shown, went out to kiss the hand of him who wore the robe. The work of the friars can be more appreciated by comparing the civilization of the Christian natives with the state of the barbarians and pagans. Whatever its defects may be, instead of the head-hunters and the idol-worshipers, the Filipino who has come within the influence of Spanish priests, though often lavish and improvident, is neat, polite, and sociable. But the friars can do better still. If they would use their influence to abolish the cock-fights Sunday afternoon, and try to co-operate more with the civil government in the matter of public education, they would find that there is plenty of work to be done yet. But some of the accusations against the friars are unfair. Extortion is a favorite charge against them; but it must be kept in mind that there are no pew-rents or voluntary contributions, and that Spain has now withdrawn the financial support that she once gave. The Church must be maintained through fees derived from weddings, funerals, and christenings. And if the Filipino, in his passion for display and splendor, orders a too expensive funeral, he has only himself, and not the priest, to blame. Indeed, the friars can derive but little benefit from a rich treasury, because, when absent from their parishes, they are allowed to have no money of their own. All of the funds remaining after the expenses of the Church are paid must be sent to the general treasury. The padre in his convent has the use of the Church money for his personal needs and charities, but nevertheless he is expected to make large returns each year. Perhaps, then, after all, the friars—Padre Pedro, anyway—are not so black as they are painted.

Chapter XV.
General Rufino in the Moro Country.

Introduction.

The story of Rufino's expedition to the Moro country in the summer of 1901 reads like a chapter from *Anabasis*. It has to do with *Capitan* Isidro's curious experiences as a hostage in the home of Datto Amay Bancurong, at Lake Lanao. It deals with the last chapter in the history of two American deserters, Morgan and Miller, of the Fortieth United States volunteers, who, under General Rufino, served as officers—soldiers of fortune in a lost campaign—and who, as a last tribute of the treachery and faithlessness of those they served, received their death-blows at the hands of Filipinos who had caught them off their guard.

The information published by Rufino shortly after his surrender has been valuable to the officers of our own army who are now exploring the mysterious interior of Mindanao. *Capitan* Isidro's intimacy with the Moros during the long period of his captivity should render his interpretation of the character, the life, and customs of this savage tribe authoritative. General Rufino, being one of the last *Insurrectos* to surrender, has not been as yet rewarded by the Government. This fact will be of consequence in case of any further outbreak on the northern coast of Mindanao. General Rufino lingers still about the scene of his exploit, and may be met with almost any time in Oroquieta, or, still better, in the sullen and revengeful village of Palilan, near the border of the Moro territory.

Rufino's Narrative.

We left Mount Liberdad on June 1, 1901, with eighteen officers, and privates to the number of four hundred and forty-two. Our destination was the town of Uato, on the shore of Lake Lanao, where, in obedience to our instructions from the Filipino *junta* at Hong Kong, we were to arrange a conference with the leading dattos in regard to an alliance of the Filipino and the Moro forces to conduct a joint campaign against the American army of invasion.

Among our officers were two deserters from I company of the Fortieth United States volunteers, Morgan and Miller, who were mere adventurers, and who desired to clear the country and embark for Africa. Morgan was supposed to have been wanted for some criminal offense in the United States. He claimed to have deserted as a consequence of punishments received by him which he considered to be undeserved. His comrade Miller followed him; but I have heard that Morgan took it hard because his friend had followed such a questionable lead. An understanding had been previously arranged between our officers and Morgan, so that when the latter left the lines at Oroquieta we received him and his comrade at Aloran, six miles north.

General Rufino in Moro Country

Captain Isidro Rillas with the Datto

Our first stop was to be at Lintogout, a station on the river by the same name, that flows into the long estuary that divides our country from the Moro territory. As you can see, our march was very rough. The mountain chain, of which Mount Liberdad, Mount Rico, and Mount Esperenza are the most important peaks, is very wild and hazardous. A few miles from the coast the country breaks into ravines and hills. There are no villages; no depots for supplies. The trails are almost imperceptible, and can be followed only by the most experienced *Montesco* guides. Back in the mountains there are many natural strongholds, which are practically inaccessible. The mountain wall, with its Plutonic cañons and precipitous descents, wrapped in a chilly fog, continually towered above us on the west.

To add to our embarrassments, we were harassed by a detachment of United States troops that had been pursuing us. Their plan was to close in upon us in two sections, from the front and rear. Near Lintogout we came to an engagement with Lieutenant Patterson's command. My army was by this time seriously crippled. We had lost one hundred and forty men the previous day by desertion. The deserting men, however, did not take their arms. Lieutenant Patterson's command must have been quite exhausted, for they camped at night on a plateau along the precipice, where an attack by us would have been inadvisable. The troops were new and untried; the experience for them was something they had not anticipated. Yet they kept at it stubbornly, slinging their carbines on their backs, and climbing up hand over hand in places where they had lost the trail. Their guides were evidently somewhat of a puzzle to them, as the Montese idea of distance is indefinite. "When I have finished this cigar we will be there," they say; and *"poco distancia"* with them means often many miles.

We were not inconvenienced much by the engagement. Our American lieutenants superintended the construction of intrenchments, back of which we lay, and fired a volley at the enemy. At their advance our army scattered, and a number of our soldiers, taking inexcusable advantage of the opportunity, deserted. On the next day we set out, reduced in numbers to two hundred and fifty-two. None of our men were killed or wounded in the fight.

We then proceeded overland to Lake Lanao, the journey occupying sixteen days, during which time the army had no rice, but had to exist entirely on the native fruits. Our tardiness in reaching Lake Lanao was caused by two attacks by Moros, June 15th. In order to avoid this enemy we made a detour, coming dangerously near the coast at Tucuran. At Tucuran three men deserted. Thence our march led inland to Bacáyan, following the south shore of the lake. Before we reached Bacáyan we were met (June 29th and 30th) by Dattos Casiang and Pindalonan, with their combined forces. Our side lost two killed, three wounded (who were taken captive); and the Moros, thirteen killed, three wounded. Arriving at Bacáyan July 1st, we waited there twelve days.

Then we set out along the south shore to Uato on the lake, which place we reached without engagement on the nineteenth of July. We stopped at Uato ten days, there borrowing $500 "Mex" from Datto Bancurong. We were obliged to leave Captain Isidro Rillas with the datto for security. The very money that we now were borrowing the Moros had received from us for their protection during our campaign, and for their promising not to molest us all the time that we were in their territory. Having loaned us money, they now sold us rice, in which negotiation, just as in the former one, they took advantage of our helplessness. The deal, however, was a necessary one, because the army had been for a long time without funds or rations. Leaving Uato we proceeded to Liángan, on the north coast, opposite Tudela (on the Jolo Sea). We left the Moro country on the recommendation of the two American deserters, who had been dissatisfied for some time at the turn affairs were taking.

We were attacked the first day out of Uato by the combined forces of three powerful dattos, who had previously borrowed rifles from us on the pretext of desiring to kill game. The engagement lasted until sunset. Of the Moros, ten were killed and many wounded. Night coming on, the enemy withdrew for re-enforcements. They returned the next day several thousand strong, and would have utterly annihilated us (for we were worn by fever and starvation) had it not been for Datto Bandia's advice, which finally discouraged the attack.

We reached Liangan July 31st with two hundred and thirty-nine men. Here we purchased rifles from the Moros, crossed the bay at night, and reached Tudela August 5th. Procrastination on the part of the conferring dattos made a failure of the expedition. We had spent about $10,000 gold for rations, good will, and protection.

Morgan and Miller, when the army was disbanded, lived around Langaran for a while. One day while they were bathing in the sea, they were cut-down by natives—I do not know why. Morgan was killed while arguing with his assailants. "We have done a lot for you," he said; but those were his last words. Miller, attempting to escape by running through the shallow water, was pursued by *bancas* and dispatched. The bodies were found later in a marsh.

Capitan Isidro Rillas's Narrative.

I was to have been educated for the Church; but after studying for some time in Cebu preparatory to a course at Rome, I set aside the wishes of my parents, who desired that I become a Jesuit, and took unto myself a wife.

You wonder, probably, why we Visayans, who are very peaceable, should have assumed a hostile attitude toward the Americans. Of course, we do not really like the game of war. But what positions would we hold among our own communities if we were to be easily imposed upon? You would have thought it a queer army that assembled at Mount Liberdad in 1901,—barefooted *hombres, ignorantes* from the rice-pads and the hemp-fields, armed with cutlasses and bolos—for we had no more than fifty guns— undisciplined and without military knowledge. But the appearance of your army in the war of Independence caused amusement to the British soldiers—for awhile? The Government generously recognized a number of the leaders of the insurrection, and in doing so has not done wrong. Our leaders are to-day, among our people, what your patriots are in your own land. And even you have no respect for those who hid themselves among the women during the affair at Oroquieta. Left alone, we could soon organize our government, our schools, and army. But, of course, conditions render this impossible, and so we think American protection is the best.

You ask for some account of my experiences with the Moros during our excursion to their territory. Our army was at first about five hundred strong, but nearly half the men deserted on the way. We had not counted on so much hostility among the Moros, although they are ancient enemies of ours, and until very recently have raided our coast villages and carried off our people into slavery. But when we wanted slaves, we purchased them—young Moros—from their parents at Misamis.

Though our mission was an altogether friendly one, our hosts did not let any opportunity go by of taking an unfair advantage of us. General Rufino was obliged to leave me as a hostage at Uato at the home of Datto Bancurong.

If we could have effected an alliance with the Moros, it would no doubt have been a formidable one. The Moros are well armed and expert fighting men. Most of our weapons have been purchased from them, as they had formerly acquired a stock of stolen Spanish guns. Those living in the Lake Lanao vicinity must have about two thousand Remington and Mauser guns, besides a number of old-fashioned cannon, which are mounted in their forts. They manufacture their own ammunition, which is necessarily of an indifferent quality.

We told the Moros that they would all have to work if the Americans should come. We knew that they were all slaveholders and ladrones; we knew that while they kept their slaves they would not need to work; and so we thought our argument ought to appeal to them.

When I was left with Datto Bancurong, security for the five hundred *pesos* that Rufino had been forced to borrow, I was treated with considerable hospitality. At one time when I had the fever, he secured some chickens for me,—they were very scarce. The datto had three wives, but one of them was rather old. I did not notice any ornaments of gold upon them. They wore silver rings and bracelets, which the native jewelers had made. The women are industrious, and consequently do most of the work. They are quite skillful with the loom, and manufacture from the native fabric, *ampic* (sashes) which their husbands wear. But for themselves they buy a cheaper fabric from the *Chinos*, which they dye in brilliant colors and make into blankets. You would probably mistake the men for women at first sight because of their peculiar cast of features. They are dressed much better and more picturesquely than the women, wearing bright silk turbans, sashes with gay fringe, and blouses often fancifully colored and secured by brass or mother-of-pearl buttons.

The Moro tribes, because they recognize no ruler but the local datto, are unable to accomplish anything of national significance. Concerted action is with them impossible. Thirty or forty villages are built around the lake. They are so thickly grouped, however, that one might as well regard them all as one metropolis. The mountains form a background for the lake, which is located on a high plateau. The climate here is more suggestive of a temperate zone than of a place within four hundred miles of the equator, and the nights are often disagreeably cold. To become a datto it is only necessary to possess a few slaves, wives, and carabao. A minor datto averages about four slaves, a dozen head of cattle, and two wives. He wears silk clothes, and occupies the largest *nipa* house.

The Moro weapons are of several kinds, — the *puñal* (a wedge-bladed knife), the *campalon* (a long broadsword), and the *sundang* (a Malay kriss). They also use head-axes, spears, and dirks. Being Mohammedans, they show a fatalistic bravery in battle. It is a disgrace to lose the weapon when in action; consequently it is tied to the hand. Many of their knives were made by splitting up the steel rails laid at Iligan. The brass work of the Spanish locomotives, also, was a great convenience in the manufacture of their cutlery.

Although they have schools for the boys, the Moro people do not make a speciality of education. The young men are taught from the Koran by priests, who also teach the art of making characters in Arabic. Their music is for the most part religious, inharmonious, and unmelodious. The *coluctang*, their most important instrument, resembles our guitar. They seem to recognize three grades of priests — the *emam*, the *pandita*, and the *sarip*, named in order of superiority. Their churches are great, circular inclosures, made of *nipa* and bamboo, with no attempt at decoration. Sacred instrumental music is supplied by bells and drums. The drum at Uato, where I was, being of extraordinary size, required two men to operate it. Each town contains a large percentage of ladrones, whose influence is offset by the *pandita* (or elders), three or five for every *barrio*. These are the secondary priests, and it is necessary that they go into the church three times a day to pray. At sunrise, at midday, and at sunset they will cry repeatedly, "*Aláh! Aláh! Bocamad soro-la!*" (Allah is god; Mohammed, prophet.) All the priests wear bright robes like the dattos, but the clergy is distinguished by a special *bangcala*, or turban, which is ornamented by a string of silver rings.

There are about five hundred Filipinos living with the Moros, mostly slaves. Deer, jungle-cock, wild hogs, and cattle are to be found in the plains and forests near the lake. The soil is fertile, and sufficient crops of corn, rice, coffee, and tobacco may be raised, *Camotes* (wild potatoes), fruits, and cocoanuts are very scarce.

Though many of the dattos are disposed to treat the Americans as friends, three in particular will entertain a different attitude. These are Bayang, Mario, and Taraia, who, among them, have control of many men. They realize, however, that the new invaders will be harder to oppose than were the Spaniards of the former *laissez faire* régime. The Filipinos will, of course, be glad to see the Moros beaten in the conflict that is now inevitable.

To conclude my narrative, we finally got the better of our hosts, the enemy. The Moros wanted $1,500 in return for the $500 they had loaned Rufino. "Then you must let the hostage come to his own people," said Rufino, "so that he can use his influence among them and solicit funds; for otherwise we will not ransom him." The situation did not look so very bright for me; but at a conference of the interested dattos they reluctantly decided that I might depart. Eight Moros were appointed to accompany me as a body-guard. On reaching Iligan it was requested that the post commander furnish me an escort back to Oroquieta, which was done. The Moros profited so much by our excursion, selling us good will and rice, that I am sure they will forgive us for not paying them the ransom money, which is no more than the brokerage on a small loan.

Chapter XVI.
Along the Iligan-Marahui Road.

The recent victories achieved by Captain Pershing over the fanatic More tribes in the vicinity of Lake Lanao, have opened up for military occupation a new territory equal in fertility and richness to the famous Cagayan valley of Luzon. The Moros under the American administration will be recognized as independent tribes, and be restricted probably to reservations similar to those the Indians now occupy. This means that a great tract of land will some day be thrown open for American development. The soil will yield abundant crops of corn, tobacco, coffee, rice, and other products, while the forest wealth appeals to the imagination. Rubber, sugar, hemp, and *copra* are the natural products of the country near the coast. The lake itself is situated on a high plateau, with a prevailing temperate climate. Where the mountains do not intervene, the land slopes gradually down to the sea.

One of the most important military operations that was ever undertaken in the Philippines was the construction of the Iligan-Marahui road, which, having been for some time open to the pack-trains and the heavy traffic, is at present nearing its completion. Though the work was planned by members of the engineers' corps, all the clearing, grading, and the filling-in were done by soldiers who had never until then known what it meant to handle pick and shovel. The younger officers, who, for the first time in their lives, were superintending a construction job, went out and bossed the gangs as well as many an experienced and seasoned foreman could have done. The soldiers, who deserve no little credit for their work, are members of the Twenty-eighth and the Tenth infantries.

It was about the last of January that I made a trip to Iligan, arriving in a Moro sailboat from another port on the north coast of Mindanao. Two or three army transports, with the quarantine flag flying (for the cholera was still in evidence), lay quietly at anchor in the bay. Along the shore a warm breeze ruffled the green branches of the *copra* palms. Near the new dock a gang of Moros were at work, perspiring in the hot rays of the tropic sun. A tawny group of soldiers, dressed in khaki, rested in the shade of a construction-house, and listened dreamily to far-off bugle calls.

The Moros were dressed picturesquely in a great variety of costume, ranging from bright-colored silk to dirty corduroy. Red *buya*-juice, was leaking from the corners of their mouths. Their turbans, though disgracefully unclean, were silk. Their coats were fastened by brass military buttons, and their sashes, green and red, with a long fringe, were tied around their waists; their trousers, like a pair of riding breeches, buttoned up the side.

While spending the first evening at the club, I had seen mingling with the young lieutenants, immaculate in their new olive uniforms, bronzed, mud-bespattered officers in the blue army shirt and khaki, with the Colt's six-shooter hanging from an ammunition belt. These were the strangers from the town of white tents on the border of the woods. At midnight possibly, or even later, they would mount their horses and go riding through the night to the encampment on the hill. The very next day one of the immaculate lieutenants, laying off the olive uniform, might have to don the old campaign hat and the flannel shirt, and follow his unshaven comrades up the road.

We stretched our army cots that night in the roulette room (this is not a country of hotels), and to the rattle of the balls and the monotonous drone of the croupier, "'teen and the red wins," dropped off to sleep. On the day following the *Dr. Hans* dropped in with Generals Wade and Sumner, and the jingle of the cavalry was heard as they rode out with mounted escort to inspect the operations of the road. After a dance and a reception at the residence of the commanding officer in honor of the visitors, "guard mount," the social feature of the day, was viewed from the pavilion in the little plaza where the exercise takes place. Its dignity was sadly marred that evening when a Moro datto, self-important in an absurd, overwhelming hat, accompanied by an obedient old wife on a moth-eaten Filipino pony, and a dog, ignoring everybody, jogged along the street and through the lines.

I walked out to the camp next morning with Lieutenant Harris. Even for this short stretch the road was not considered altogether safe. We forded the small river just beyond the cavalry corral, where an old

Spanish blockhouse stands, and where a few old-fashioned Spanish cannon still lie rusting in the grass. A Moro fishing village—now a few deserted shacks around the more pretentious dwelling of the former datto—may be met near where the roadway joins the beach. Pack-trains of army mules, with their armed escorts, passed us; then an ambulance, an escort wagon, and a mounted officer.

Two companies of the Tenth infantry were camped in a small clearing near the sea. Leaving the camp, we went along the almost indistinguishable Moro trail to where the mighty Agus River plunges in a greenish torrent over an abrupt wall into the deep, misty cavern far below. The rushing of the waters guided us in places where we found the trail inadequate. Arriving at the falls, we scrambled down by means of vines until we reached a narrow shelf near where the cataract began its plunge. Upon the opposite side an unyielding precipice was covered with a damp green coat of moss and fern. It took five seconds for a falling stone to reach the seething cloud of mist below.

A Deserted Moro Shack

Moro Weapons (Spear and Dirk)

The trail back to the camp was very wild. It led through jungles of dense underbrush, where monkeys scolded at us, and where wild pigs, with startled grunts, bolted precipitously for the thicket. A deep ravine would be bridged by a fallen tree. The Iligan-Marahui road now penetrates the wildest country in the world, and the most wonderful. Turning abruptly from the coast about five miles from Iligan, it winds among the rocky hills through forests of mahogany and ebony, through jungles of rattan and young bamboo, and spanning the swift Agus River with a modern steel bridge, finally connects the lake and sea. It has been built to meet the military road from the south coast, thus making possible, for the first time, communication *via* the interior. The new roads practically follow the old Moro trails.

The scene at early morning on the road was one of great activity. Soon after reveille the men are mustered, armed with picks and shovels in the place of the more customary "Krag," and long before the tropic sun has risen over the primeval woods, the chatter of monkeys and the crow of jungle-cock is mingled with the crash of trees, the click of shovels and the rumble of the dump-cart. The continued blasting on the upper road, near the "Point of Rocks," disturbs the colonies of squawking birds that dart into the forest depths like flashes of bright color. As the land is cleared for fifty yards on either side in order to admit the sunlight and to keep the Moras at a proper range, the great macao-trees, with their snaky, parasitic vines, on crashing to the ground, dislodge the pallid fungi and extraordinary orchids from their heavy foliage. Deep cuts into the clayey soil sometimes bisect whole galleries of wonderful white ants, causing untold consternation to the occupants.

Each squad of soldiers was protected by a guard besides the officer, who, armed with a revolver, acted as the overseer. The work was very telling on the men, and often out of a whole company not more than twenty-eight reported. Some grew as strong as oxen under this unusual routine; others had to take advantage of the sick report. The soldiers were required to work five hours a day, and double time after a day of rain. Considerable Moro labor was employed on the last sections of the road.

A unique feature of the work was the erection of small bridges made of solid logs from the material at hand, and bolted down by long steel bars. The "elbow" bridge which makes a bend along the hillside near the first camp is a triumph in the engineering line. The camps were moved on as the work progressed, and the advance guard ran considerable risk. The Moros had an unexpected way of visiting the scene of operation, and admiring it from certain hiding-places in the woods. As they could hike their thirty or forty miles a day along the trails, they often came much nearer to the troops than was suspected. Sentry duty was especially a risky one, as frequently at night the Moros used to fire into the camp. Only about one hundred yards along the trail a soldier, who had gone into the woods for a "short cut," received one from a Moro who was waiting for him in the shadow of a tree.

The camp at night, illuminated by the blue light of the stars, the forest casting inky shadows on the ground, seemed like some strange, mysterious domain. The officers around the tent of the commanding officer were singing songs, accompanied by the guitar and mandolin. The soldiers also from a distant tent—it was their own song, and the tune "The Girl I Left Behind Me"—practicing close harmony, began:

> "O, we're camped in the sand in a foreign land
>   Near the mighty Agus River,
> With the brush at our toes, the skeeters at our nose,
>   The jimjams and the fever.
>
> We're going up to Lake Lanao,
>   To the town they call Marahui;
> When the road is built and the Moros killed,
>   We'll none of us be sorry.
>
> We're blasting stumps and grading bumps;
>   Our arms and backs are sore, O!
> We work all day just a dreamin' of our pay,
>   And d——n the husky Moro!

When taps sounded, we turned in beneath two blankets in a wall-tent lighted by a feeble lantern. All night long the restless jungle sounds, the whispering of the mysterious forest, and the distant booming of the sea, together with the measured tread of the night sentry, made a lullaby which ought to have worked wonders with the "jim-jam" and the fever patients of the Twenty-eighth.

Chapter XVII.
The Filipino at Play.

As in the pre-Elizabethan days the public amusements consisted of performances by priests and monks on scaffolding set up before the church, mystery plays, "moralities," and "miracles," religious pageants through the village streets,—so in the Philippines, where they have not outlived the fourteenth century, the Church plays an important part in popular *fiestas*. The Christmas holidays are celebrated still by carol singing from house to house, and by the presentation of the old-time "mystery" by strolling bands of actors, with a wax-doll to represent the Sacred Child.

Each town, besides the regular church holidays—as indicated by innumerable red marks in the calendar—has a *fiesta* for its patron saint, which is of more importance even than the "Feast of Aguinaldo" ("Aguinaldo" is their word for "Christmas present"), which is held annually in December. One of these *fiestas* is announced by the ringing of the church-bells—big bells and little bells all turning somersaults, and being banged as they go round. During the intermissions the municipal band discourses Spanish and Visayan music, coming to the end with a triumphant bang. Only on Holy Friday are the bells abandoned and tin pans and bamboo clappers, sticks and stones, resorted to for purposes of lamentation— functions for which these instruments are perfectly adapted.

People come in from far and near, riding in *bancas* or on ponies, often spending several nights upon the way. The great church at the morning mass is crowded; women faint; and, as the heat increases, it becomes a steaming oven. It is more spectacular at vespers, with the women kneeling among the goats and dogs; the men, uncovered, standing in the shadows of the gallery; the altar sparkling with a hundred candles; and the dying sunlight filtering through mediæval windows. As the resinous incense odor fills the house, through the wide-open doors the sun can be seen setting in its tropical magnificence behind a grove of palms.

Then the procession, in a haze of dust—led by the band, the padre, and the acolytes; the sacred relics borne aloft on floats encircled by a blaze of candles; young men holding each other's hands; children and old women following, holding their tapers and reciting prayers—files through the streets to the eternal clamor of the bells.

The afternoon is given up to tournaments—carabao races, pony races, *banca* races, cock-fights. Bamboo arches, decorated with red banners, are erected in the larger thoroughfares, and under these the horsemen ride together at full tilt, attempting to secure upon their lances the suspended rings which are the favors of the local *señoritas*. On dropping in at that volcanic little town, Mambajo, one hot afternoon, I found a goose hung up upon the bamboo framework which became the property of the competitor who, riding under it *ventre á terre*, could seize the prize, regardless of the feelings of the goose. The village had turned out in holiday attire, as the dense atmosphere of cocoanut-oil and perfumery proclaimed. The band, in white pith helmets and new linen uniforms, was playing under the mimosa-tree. Down the main road a struggling crowd of wheelmen came, and from a cloud of dust the winner of the mile bicycle-race shot past the tape. The difficulty in the carabao event was to stick on to the broad, clumsy animal, during the gallop around the course. One of the beasts, excited by the shouts, began to run amuck, and cut a swathe in the distracted crowd as clean as an ungovernable automobile might have made.

The ringing of a bell announced the cock-fight in the main beneath the cocoanut-trees. It was near the market-place, where venders of betel-nut, tobacco, cigarettes, and *tuba* squatted on the ground, their wares exposed for sale on mats. As the spectators crowded in, the gatekeeper would mark their bare feet with a red stamp, indicating that admission had been paid. On booths arranged within the last inclosure, *señoritas* sold hot chocolate and raisin-cakes and beer. Tethered to little stakes, and straining at their leashes, the excited game-cocks, the descendants of the jungle-fowl, screamed in exultant unison. The small boys, having climbed the cocoanut-palms, clung to the notches, and looked down upon the scene of conflict.

Little brown men, squatting around the birds, were critically hefting them, or matching couples of them in preliminary bouts, keeping a good hold of their tails. There was the wicked little Moro

Bangcorong, the trainer of birds that never lost a fight. There was Manolo, the Visayan dandy, who on recent winnings in the main, supported a small stable of racing ponies at Cebu. The person entering a bird deposits a certain amount of money with the bank. This wager is then covered by the smaller bets of *hoi poiloi*. When a "dark" bird is victorious, and the crowd wins, an enthusiastic yell goes up. But just as in a public lottery, fortune is seldom with the great majority. As the bell rings, the spectators press close around the bamboo pit, or climb to points of vantage in adjacent scaffolding. A line is drawn in the damp earth, and on one side all the money wagered on the favorite is arranged, which must be balanced by the coin placed by opposing betters on the other side. There is a frantic rushing around at the last moment to place bets. The Chinaman waves a ten-*peso* bill excitedly, and clamors "*buenting! buenting!*" — meaning that he puts his money on the speckled bird. Somebody on the other side cries out "*guingan!*" or "green," and thus they both find takers for their "*sapi.*" Then the *presidente*, who referees the fight, sends two policemen to clear out the ring; the sheaths are removed from the razor-sharp steel spurs; the two cocks are held opposite each other, and are simultaneously launched into the arena. Ruffling, and facing each other with their necks outstretched, "blood in their eyes," and realizing to the full extent the danger of the situation, they prepare to fight it out to death. A quick stab, and the victim, trembling violently, a stream of red blood trickling down its leg, drops at the first encounter, and the fight is over.

While no record has been kept of how the bets were placed, every one seems to remember, and the money is handed over honestly. If Filipinos were as honorable in all their dealings as they are in this, they would be ideal people to do business with; for although they will beg and borrow, or even steal, to get the money which is wagered at these "combats," they will never evade a debt of honor thus incurred. Regarding gambling as a livelihood, or a profession in good standing, they devote their best hours to the study and the mastery of it. They, with their false philosophy, believe that wealth is thus produced, and that there is a gain for every one.

The list of fights progresses, some of the cocks only giving up the struggle after a last dying kick has been directed at the breast of the antagonist, who, desperately wounded, summons strength for one triumphant, but a rather husky, crow. Sometimes both birds are taken from the cockpit dead. The bird that loses a fight through cowardice is rent limb from limb by the indignant owner, and is ignominiously hung upon the bamboo paling,—bird of ill omen, that has ruined the finances of a family, mortgaged the house and carabao, and plunged its owner into debt for the next year!

Sometimes a "free for all" is substituted for the dual contest. Eighteen or twenty fighting-cocks will be arranged in a large circle, dropped at the same time in the ring, and set to work. Half of the birds, not realizing what is going on, will innocently start to scratch for worms, or set out on a search for seeds. It is amusing then to see the astonished look they give when suddenly confronted by a couple of antagonists. They settle their disputes in bunches of three and four, and soon the ring is full of chickens running to get out of danger, maimed and crippled, or still innocently scratching after worms. There was a little white cock at the recent main at Oroquieta, who avoided every fight without, however, leaving the arena. The game old buzzard that belonged to *Capitan* A-Bey—a bird with legs like stilts and barren patches in his foliage—had put down every challenger in turn. Confronted by two birds at once, he seemed to say, "One side, old fellow, for a moment; will attend to your case later"—which he did. Dizzy and staggering from loss of blood, still "in the ring," he sidled up to the immaculate white bird that had so ingeniously evaded every fight. It was a case of out-and-out bluff. If the little bird had struck, he must have won. A single look, however, at his reprehensible antagonist sufficed. The little bird made a direct line for the gate, while *Capitan* A-Bey's old rooster, with defiance in his look and voice, was carried away in triumph. In the parade next day, where the competing game-cocks were exhibited, the "buzzard," though he was exempt from taking part in the proceedings, led the procession and was loudly cheered.

My introduction to polite society in Filipinia was certainly auspicious. "Betel-Nut Sal," the wife of the constabulary sergeant, had a birthday, and invited everybody to the dance and the reception which would take place in the jail. The *Señorita* Tonio, most prominent of the receiving ladies, was engaged when I arrived, in meting out gin to the visitors. Her teeth were red from betel-chewing, and a cigarette hung from the corner of her mouth. The orchestra, armed with guitars and mandolins, had seated themselves upon a bench, barefooted with their legs crossed, ready to begin. The insufficiency of partners for the ladies had necessitated letting out most of the prisoners on parole. A certain young dandy who had been locked up on charge of murder, was the hero of the hour. While he was dancing, soldiers with their Remingtons guarded the door. I was induced to try a dance with Tonio. The hum of music could be heard above the "clack-clack" of the carpet-slippers tapping on the floor. Then suddenly the *señorita* swore a white man's oath, and stopped. Her carpet-slipper had come off, and as she wore no hosiery, the situation was indeed embarrassing. Our hostess asked us twenty times if everything was satisfactory, and finally confessed that she had spent almost a year's income for the refreshments. "Dancee now; *mañana*, washie, washie."

I must tell you of Bernarda's party. "We expect you for the eating," read the invitation, and when dinner was all ready I was sent for. Then we sat down to a feast of roast pork, rice, and goat-flesh, with a rather soggy cake for the dessert. At most balls it is customary for the ladies to be seated first at the refreshment-table, where the most substantial articles of diet are boiled ham with sugar frosting, cakes flavored with the native lime, and lemon soda. Like the coy nun in Chaucer's "Prologue," she who is most elegant will take care not to spill the food upon her lap, eat with the fingers, or spit out the bones. At wedding feasts the gentlemen are given preference at the table.

When the orchestra arrived—a trifle late after a six-mile hike through muddy roads and over swollen streams—the company was more delighted than a nursery. The orchestra began the program with the piece entitled "Just One Girl," to which the people sang Visayan words. Vivan, the old clown, in clumsy commissary shoes, skated around the floor to the amusement of the whole assembly. The chair-dance was announced, and the most favored *señorita* occupied a chair set in the middle of the room. A dozen suitors came in order, bowing low, entreating her not to reject their plea. One after another they were thrown down, and retired crestfallen. But at last the right one came, and waltzed off with the girl triumphantly. There was a salvo of applause, the more intense because in this case an engagement had been practically announced. No native ball would be complete without the symbolistic dance which so epitomizes Filipino character. This is performed by a young lady and her partner wielding fans and scented handkerchiefs, advancing and retreating with all kinds of coquetries.

Long after midnight, when the party broke up with the customary horse-play, the accommodating orchestra, who had enjoyed the evening with the rest, still playing "Just One Girl," escorted the assembly home.

Chapter XVIII.
Visayan Ethics and Philosophy.

He is the drollest little person in the world—the Filipino of the southern isles. He imitates the sound of chickens in his language and the nasal "nga" of the carabao. He talks about his chickens and makes jokes about them. As he goes along the street, he sings, "*Ma-ayon buntag*," or "*Ma-ayon hapon*," to the friends he meets. This is his greeting in the morning and the afternoon; at night, "*Ma-ayon gabiti*." And instead of saying, "Thank you," he will sing, "*Deus mag bayud*" (God will reward you), and the answer, also sung, will be "*gehapon*" (always)—just as though it were no use to look for a reward upon this world.

You wonder how it is that he can spend his life rooted to one spot, like a tree, passing the days in idleness. He is absorbed in his own thoughts. If you should ask him anything he would not hear you; he is far away in his own dreamland. You must wake him up first, and then repeat your question several times. If you should have instructions for him, do not give them to him all at once. A single idea at a time is all that he can carry in his head. If he has not been broken in to a routine, he will chase butterflies upon the way, influenced ever by the passion of the moment. There is no yesterday or no to-morrow in his thoughts. What he shall find to eat to-morrow never concerns him. Sufficient unto the day is the evil thereof.

Many mistakes have been made in the hasty judgment of the Filipino character. Such axioms as "Never trust a native under any circumstances;" "Never expect to find a sense of gratitude;" "Never believe a word a native says," are only too well known in Filipinia. The Spanish influence has been responsible for most of the defects as well as for the merits of the native character. Then, the peculiar fashion of the Oriental mind forbids his reasoning according to the Occidental standards. Cause and effect are hazy terms to him, and the justification of the means is not regarded seriously. His thefts are in a way consistent with his system of philosophy. You are so rich, and he so poor. The Filipino is at heart a socialist. But he does not steal indiscriminately. If it is your money that he takes, it is because he needs it to put up on the next cock-fight. If he selects your watch, it is because he needs a watch, and nothing more. The Filipino, when he transacts business, has two scales of prices,—one for the natives, and another for Americans. He reasons that because Americans are rich, they ought to pay a higher price for what they get than Filipinos do. He would expect if he bought anything from you that you would make a special rate for him regardless of the value of the article in question. You would have to come down to accommodate his pocketbook.

The Filipino code of ethics justifies a falsehood, especially if the end in view should be immediate. He lies to save himself from punishment, and he will make a cumulative lie, building it up from his imagination until even the artistic element is wanting, and his lie becomes a thing of contradictions and absurdities. When questioned closely, or when cross-examined, his imagination gets beyond control, and it is possible that he believes, himself, the "fairy tales" he tells. Fear easily upsets his calculations, and he runs amuck. But he will not betray himself, although he will deny a friend three times. He may be in an agony of fear, but only by the subtlest changes could it be detected.

The Spaniards, when they left out gratitude from his curriculum, made up for the deficiency by inculcating strict ideals of discipline. The Filipino never has had much to be grateful for, and he regards a friendly move suspiciously. But he admires a master, and will humbly yield to almost any kind of tyranny, especially from one of his own race. The poorer classes rather like to be imposed upon in the same way as the Americans appreciate a humbug.

In their communities the *presidente* is supreme in power; and, like the king, this officer can do no wrong. He uses his position for his private ends. Why not? What is the use of being *presidente* if it does not profit you? I have known some who secured monopolies on the hemp-trade by fining all who did not sell their hemp to them. Others appropriate the public funds for entertainment purposes, and when an inquiry is made regarding the condition of the treasury, the magistrate expresses the greatest surprise on finding that there is no money left. This officer, however, whatever his prerogatives may be, is not ambitious that his term of office be of any benefit. If he presides well at the cock-fights, it is all that is expected of him. If he goes to building bridges over rivers that the horses easily can wade across, the people will object to the unnecessary labor and expense. The *presidente* dominates the town. If he can bring about prosperity in an agreeable way, without recourse to sudden means, the people will appreciate him and support him, though they do not take much interest in the elections. If the civil government can only get good *presidentes* in the larger villages, the problem of administration will be solved.

Malay traditions make the Filipino proud, disdainful, and reserved—and also cruel. Not only are the ardent sun and his inherent laziness accountable for his antipathy to work. It is beneath his dignity to work, and that is why he takes delight in being a public servant or a clerk. The problem of living is reduced to simplest terms. One can not starve to death as long as the bananas and the cocoanuts hold out. The question as to whether last year's overcoat or straw hat can be made to do, does not concern the Filipino in the least. If he needs money irresistibly, he can spend one day at work up in the mountains, making enough to last him for some time. If he can spend his money so as to create a display, he takes delight in doing so. But paying debts is as uninteresting as it is unpopular. The outward signs of elegance are much respected by the Filipino. The American, to live up to his part, must always be attended by a servant. Sometimes, when we would forget this adjunct, we would stop at some *tienda* and propose to carry home a dozen eggs wrapped in a handkerchief. "What! have you no house-boy?" the natives asked. Apparently extravagant, they practice many petty economies at home. A morsel of food or a bit of clothing never goes to waste in Filipinia. They imitate the Chinaman in letting one of their finger-nails grow long.

The Filipino is fastidious and dainty—in his own way. He will shudder at the uncouth Tagalog who toasts locusts over a hot fire and eats them, and that evening will go home and eat a handful of damp *guinimos*, the littlest of fish. He takes an infinite amount of care of his white clothes, and swaggers about the streets immaculate; but just as soon as he gets home, the suit comes off and is reserved for future exhibition purposes. The women pay comparatively small attention to their personal adornment. Their hair is combed straight back upon their heads. The style of dresses never undergoes a change. The ordinary dress consists of three important pieces—the chemise, a long, white, sleeveless garment; the *camisa*, or the *piña* bodice, with wide sleeves; and the skirt, caught up on one side, and preferably of red material. A yoke or scarf of *piña* folds around the neck, and is considered indispensable by *señoritas*. The native ideas of modesty are more or less false, varying with the individual.

It might be thought that, on account of his indifferent attitude toward life and death, the Filipino has no feelings or emotions. He is a stoic and a fatalist by nature, but an emotionalist as well. While easily affected, the impressions are not deep, and are forgotten as they slip into the past. Although controlled by passion, he will hold himself in, maintaining a proud reserve, especially in the presence of Americans. A subtle change of color, a sullen brooding, or persistent silence, are his only outward signs of wrath. He will endure in patience what another race had long ago protested at; but when at last aroused and dominated by his passions, he will throw reserve and caution to the winds, and give way to his feelings like a child; and like a child, he feels offended if partiality is exercised against him. His sense of justice then asserts itself, and he resents not getting his share of anything. He even will insist on being punished if he thinks punishment is due him. While revengeful if imposed upon, and bitter under the autocracy of cruelty, he has a great respect for firmness. And the Americans would do well to remember that in governing the Filipino, kindness should be mingled with strict discipline.

The Filipino can not be depended upon for accurate, reliable information. His information is indefinite, as perhaps it should be in the land of By and By. In spite of his imaginative temperament, his cruelty to animals is flagrant. He starves his dog and rides his pony till the creature's back is sore. He shows no mercy for the bird that loses at the cock-fight; he will mercilessly tear it limb from limb. In order to explain—not to excuse—this cruelty, we must again regard the Filipino as a child—a child of the toad-stabbing age.

A little learning he takes seriously, and is puffed up by pride when he can follow with his horny finger the religious column in *Ang Suga*, spelling the long words out laboriously. Even the boys and girls who study English, often do so only to be "smart." It is a clever thing to spice one's conversation with an English word or expression here and there.

Yet the Filipino is not altogether lazy and unsympathetic. Often around his houses you will see a tiny patch of corn or a little garden of green vegetables. He makes a mistake by showing a dislike for the *camote*, or the native sweet-potato, which abounds there. Preferring the unsubstantial rice to this more wholesome product, he leaves the sweet-potato for his Chinese and his Moro neighbors. On every street the sour-smelling *copra* (cocoanut meat) can be seen spread out upon a mat to dry. The cattle are fed on the long rice-grass (the *palay*), or on the unhusked rice (*sacate*). A primitive trades-unionism exists among the Filipinos; every trade, such as the carpenters' or the musicians', having its respective *maestro*, with whom arrangements for the labor and the pay are always made. The native jewelers are very clever, fashioning the silver *pesos* into ornaments for bolos, hats, or walking-sticks. Ironmongeries, though primitive in their equipment, have produced, by dint of skill and patience, work that is very passable. The women weave their own cloth on the native looms, and practice various other industries. The children are well trained in hospitality and public manners, which they learn by rote.

While not original, they are good imitators, and would make excellent clerks, mechanics, carpenters, or draughtsmen. Some of their devices rather remind one of a small boy's remedy for warts or "side-ache." In order to exterminate the rats they introduce young pythons into the garrets of their houses, where the snake remains until his appetite is satisfied for rodents and his finer tastes developed. Usually the Filipino does things "wrong side out." Instead of beckoning when he would summon any one, he motions away from himself. Instead of making nicknames, such as Bob or Bill, from the first syllable, he uses the last, abbreviating Balendoy to 'Doy, Diega to a simple 'Ga. They are the happiest people in the world, free from all care and trouble. It is among the younger generation that the promise lies. The little ones are bright and gentle and respectful—quite unlike the boisterous denizens of Young America. The race is still back in the fourteenth century, but the progress to be made within the next few years will span the chasm at a single bound.

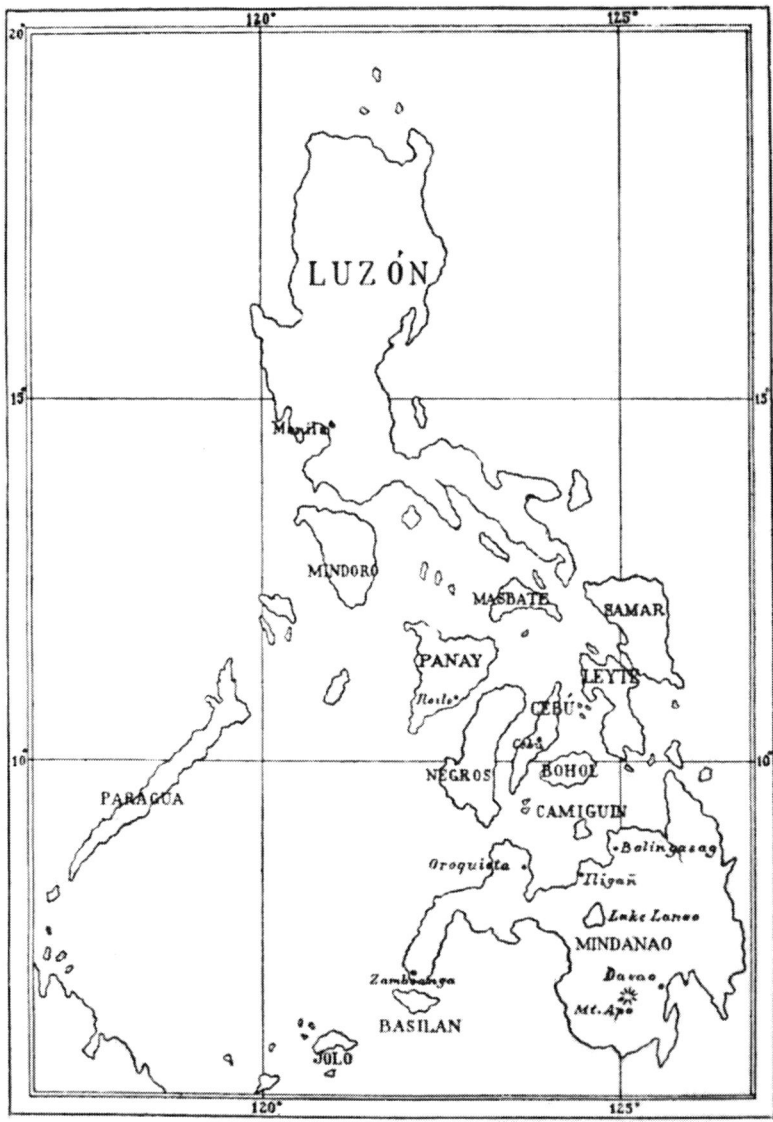

When I return to Filipinia, I shall expect to see, instead of the brown *nipa* shacks, bright-painted American cottages or bungalows among the groves of palm. I shall expect to see the mountain slopes, waving with green hemp-fields, worked by the rejuvenated native. Railroads will penetrate into the dark interior, connecting towns and villages now isolated. The country roads will be well graded and macadamized, and bridges will be built across the streams. The cock-fight will have given way to institutions more American, and superstition will have vanished with the mediævalism. The hum of saw-mills will be heard upon the borders of the timber-lands; sugar refineries will be established near the fields of cane; for Filipinia is still an undeveloped paradise. The Great White Tribe has many problems yet to solve; but with the industry that they have shown in other lands, they can improve, not only the material resources, but can stir the Filipino from his dream of the Dark Ages, and point out the way of modern progress and enlightenment.

CPSIA information can be obtained at www.ICGtesting.com
Printed in the USA
LVOW08s2111080715

445451LV00001B/237/P